D1239410

A Boy Named Jesus

A Boy Named Jesus

Robert Aron

INTRODUCTION BY
Bishop John Shelby Spong

EDITOR
Ray Riegert

Ulysses Press   Berkeley, CA
1997

Published by: Ulysses Press
P.O. Box 3440
Berkeley, CA 94703-3440

Library of Congress Catalog Card Number: 97-60152

ISBN: 1-56975-119-6

First published in hardback as *Jesus of Nazareth: The Hidden Years* by William Morris & Company

Printed in Canada by Best Book Manufacturers

10 9 8 7 6 5 4 3 2 1

Copy Editor: David Sweet
Cover Design: Big Fish
Indexer: Sayre Van Young

Distributed in the United States by Publishers Group West, in Canada by Raincoast Books, and in Great Britain and Europe by World Leisure Marketing.

Library of Congress Cataloging-in-Publication Data

Aron, Robert, 1898–1975.
    A boy named Jesus / Robert Aron; introduction by John Shelby Spong.
        p. cm.
    Rev. ed. of: Jesus of Nazareth. 1962.
    Includes index.
    ISBN 1-56975-119-6 (trade paper)
    1. Jesus Christ—Education. I Aron, Robert, 1898–1975. Jesus of Nazareth.
II. Title.
BT330.A713 1997
232.92'7—dc21   97-9424 CIP

Contents

Introduction

by John Shelby Spong
Episcopal Bishop of Newark

I am amazed at how much I enjoyed and profited from the reading of this book. This unexpected response occurred because I had misinterpreted the title to mean that this book was one more fanciful attempt to fill in the blanks in the life of Jesus. Those who typically write about the "lost years" of Jesus must have rich imaginations, for they cannot research a period for which there is absolutely no data. Speculative re-creations of childhood and young adult adventures in the supposed "lost years" in Jesus' life edify me not at all.

Even the concept of "lost years" is based upon the literalization of a biblical text that most scholars today would simply dismiss. Those years are supposed to be the time between Jesus' being taken up to Jerusalem by his parents when he was twelve years of age, a story recorded for us only by Luke (2:41-52), and his adult baptism by John the Baptist, which was supposed to have inaugurated his public ministry and which Luke, at least, suggests came when he was thirty years of age (Luke 3:23). So, suddenly eighteen lost years cry out for some accounting, and many a would-be author has been unable or unwilling to resist the temptation to fill in the blanks. Yet the temple visit at age twelve we now recognize to be part of the birth tradition, which is almost universally regarded today as midrashic storytelling and not history. It is in all probability a Samuel story being retold about Jesus. Furthermore, the story of Jesus' baptism, while possessing an almost certain kernel of history, is so clearly stylized to elevate Jesus and to diminish John the Baptist, that its content is also generally discounted as history.

The creative imagination of those who wish to be Jesus' biographers knows no boundaries. In the genre of books dedicated to the lost years, one can read of fascinating possibilities, such as Jesus' journey to India, his marriage and even the birth of his children. About India and his being a parent there is not a single supportive fact. The possibility that Jesus was married remains a debatable speculation. None of that kind of speculation appears in this volume. (I tried to make a case for Jesus' marriage in my book *Born of a Woman: A Bishop Rethinks the Virgin Birth and the Treatment of Women by a Male-Dominated Church*, pp. 187-199.)

Robert Aron was a popular French historian who wrote extensively in the 1950s and 1960s. He recognized, as all historians surely must, that Jesus of Nazareth was a figure of history, concrete and specific. He did not suddenly materialize as an adult in the district of Galilee. He was not, as John A. T. Robinson suggested, working from Frederick Schlermacher's image, "a cuckoo introduced into the human nest" (*The Human Face of God*, p. 43). Jesus was a human being, a particular man. As such, he had to live at a particular time. He was part of a particular people and was shaped by the particular events that affected his nation, his region and his world. He spoke a particular language, which inevitably meant that he perceived reality in a particular way, for that is the function of language. He worshiped in a particular manner. His view of God was shaped by a particular religious heritage. These and a thousand other details helped to create the person of history named Jesus of Nazareth, who broke upon the world in the early years of the first century of this common era and who started a movement that has been a major force in shaping the history of our civilization. It is certainly the task of the historian to place this life into its historical context, to discern from those things we know about him in his adulthood the various forces and the crucial influences that molded him into the person he was. That is what Robert Aron has done in this volume, and he has done it brilliantly.

Such a task, to the historian, seems like a simple and straightforward thing to do, yet in the case of Jesus of Nazareth it is a surprisingly difficult endeavor. That difficulty is created by the layers of emotion, tradition, legend, interpretation and worship that have for centuries surrounded the life of this Jesus. So deep are the religious sensitivities concerning Jesus that sometimes the simple historical question, when raised, is perceived as a personal attack on a believer's faith. The historian, as an historian, is not competent to debate the divine claims made for this Jesus. Those divine claims are, however, sometimes forced by historical research into a debate in which their excesses are challenged and thus faith anxieties are raised. That is certainly one issue that the reader must confront in this book.

A second issue that is raised by this book comes with the realization that, despite years of research, our ability to capture the essence of the Jesus of history is still quite compromised. Albert

Schweitzer, in his monumental book, *The Quest of the Historical Jesus*, published in 1906, maintained that such a search was all but impossible to carry out. Even before the Gospels were written, Jesus had been wrapped in a number of interpretive envelopes. There is no uninterpreted Jesus of history that can be found anywhere. For anyone to be able to journey behind the Gospels, which are themselves interpretive pieces of literature, is not easy.

In this century a well-known group of scholars, the Jesus Seminar, has reopened this quest for the historical Jesus with unusual vigor. Their ability to get their message and their research into the media has greatly enhanced public interest. They have also raised up vigorous opposition. Their very success, however, has had the effect of minimizing the documentary evidence upon which the picture of the Jesus of history might be created. The conclusion of the Seminar, that only eighteen percent of the words attributed to Jesus in the Gospels are authentic, has left the curious public with a database of facts so meager that Jesus is reduced to the status of a first-century Jewish sage, perhaps even a tragic/comic figure. Such a Jesus is certainly not capable of sustaining the ecclesiastical superstructure that has been built up around him. So for this reason traditional believers once again find the work of the Jesus Seminar threatening to their faith and, perhaps even more so, deeply threatening to their power.

But it is not the task of the historian to undergird the ecclesiastical superstructure. There is even among the more thoughtful adherents of religion a sense that truth might well be served by the collapse of that increasingly heavy ecclesiastical machinery. In their minds it is this very superstructure that tends to obscure the Jesus figure, preventing our interaction with him on deep and significant levels. So this becomes yet another issue that the historian searching for Jesus must face.

Whether admitted in religious circles or not, the superstructure of ecclesiastical Christianity is, in our day, clearly tottering. Its foundations have been shaken. The accuracy of the Church's interpretation of Jesus of Nazareth is widely questioned and enormous gaps in the Jesus story have been subjected to vigorous historical research. Slowly, but surely, even among believers, new questions are being formed and new conclusions are being reached. Robert Aron is one of many voices being raised in the wilderness of this moment, calling the world to find a new starting place if it wants to speak with seriousness about the Jesus who lies hidden beyond these collapsing structures. The debate is dynamic, invigorating, fearful and threatening to the securities and religious sensitivities of yesterday. But truth can never be harnessed in the service of the conclusions of the past. That is the case even for that truth for which either inerrancy or infallibility has traditionally been claimed by the Church.

Behind the structures of the past, however, behind the dogmatic theological assertions of antiquity that gave the world such concepts as "the Incarnation" and "the Holy Trinity," and even behind the interpretive portraits of Jesus drawn in the Gospels themselves, there still remains a powerful experience of God that people believed they found in the life of a first-century man named Jesus of Nazareth. Neither doctrines nor structure would have arisen apart from that experience. That experience had to be processed in typically human ways. When that interpretive process was over, a powerful institution was erected upon the foundations that the interpretations had laid. That institution in time achieved the ability to make kings and to remove them, to define life and to compel acceptance of its definitions, to create stereotypes and to enforce them, and to resist the truth whenever it threatened the institution's power. But when all of that is admitted, and even if that institution collapses in total destruction, there still remains the experience of Jesus, called Christ, which was the basis upon which all of these things originally came into being. It is this primal Christ experience that still cries out to be understood even in our age. It also beckons to be explored again and again and even to be entered anew in every generation. It is the task of the historian to find a pathway that leads us into that experience, to test its reality and to enable us to move as close to that moment as possible.

A legitimate question for the historian would be, "What was the Jesus experience?" That question lies underneath all the faith claims of antiquity. Why did one of those who was transformed by that experience in its earliest years exclaim that somehow "God was in this Christ." What was the essence of that moment that was interpreted as if it were a divine encounter? Those are the questions that still beg for answers today. Those of us who, like Robert Aron, cannot ignore this perpetual source of energy, must probe again and again the Jesus moment or the Christ experience in search of that meaning.

Aron's probe begins quite fittingly with the fact of history that Jesus of Nazareth was a Jewish man. No matter what else might be said about him, this is the place where every serious inquiry about Jesus must begin.

His name was Yeshuah, not Jesus. Jesus is a westernized version of his Jewish name. His mother's name was Miriam, not Mary. The records that we do have suggest that, as a Jewish boy, he was circumcised on the eighth day of his life (Luke 2:21), that his mother underwent the Jewish rites of purification on the fortieth day of his life (Luke 2:22-24) and that perhaps the historical kernel of truth behind that trip to Jerusalem at age twelve was a memory of a primitive kind of bar mitzvah puberty rite (Luke 2:41-52). Jesus appears to have been a frequent worshiper in the synagogue

(Mark 1:21, 23, 29; 3:1; 6:2. Matthew 12:9; 13:54. Luke 4:16; 6:6). He is remembered as one who was familiar with the sacred scriptures of his people, as well as the cultic traditions that governed both Sabbath day observance and social laws of uncleanliness (Matthew 12:2ff, 10:8; Mark 2:23ff, 5:25; Luke 4:16ff, 7:22).

The death of this Jesus was also caught up in things Jewish long before the narrative story of his crucifixion was written. Saint Paul gave voice to this reality when he wrote that Jesus "died for our sins in accordance with the scriptures" (I Corinthians 15:3). It was Paul also who seems to have placed upon Jesus' death the image of the paschal lamb (I Corinthians 5:7). "Christ, our Passover, is sacrificed for us," the Church has continued to say throughout the ages, sometimes with little or no comprehension of what those words mean. The slaying of the paschal lamb, the Jews suggested, broke the power of death during the trauma of the Exodus in Jewish history (Exodus 12). When the Jews escaped their bondage of slavery, they recalled that moment liturgically by sprinkling the blood of the paschal lamb on the doorposts of their Jewish homes and by retelling the story of their deliverance. That original action, according to the biblical text, had caused the promised plague, which involved the death of the first-born of each household to fall only on Egyptian households. The blood of the Passover, it was said, had deterred the angel of death from afflicting Jewish homes. In the liturgical setting after the moment of deliverance had been observed, the family then proceeded to consume the lamb in a celebratory feast.

Now observe how these Jewish symbols were used by the earliest disciples, who were all Jewish, to interpret the death of Jesus of Nazareth. Jesus was referred to as God's first-born son who was slain, a clear reference to the Passover story. In time he came to be thought of as a substitute for the paschal lamb. In the Jesus story the bondage of the people was interpreted, not as the bondage of slavery as it was in the time of the first Passover, but as the bondage to sin. The cross was understood as forming the doorposts of the world, upon which the blood of the paschal victim was sprinkled so that the power of death would be broken eternally. Finally, when their deliverance was secured and appropriately observed liturgically, the redeemed of God would celebrate their victory by consuming, in a liturgical feast, the body and blood of this new paschal lamb. None of these symbols of the Christian story make sense if they are separated from the Jewish interpretive frame of reference. Yet with almost no comprehension of Jewish liturgical practice, these themes have become a standard part of Christianity.

The death of Jesus, understood as something done "for our sins," called other Jewish images into the story of the cross. These images have also been lodged in our church liturgies. Once again, however, they have been continued with little or no meaning for those who do not understand the Jewish interpretive context that had been wrapped around Jesus. For example, what could possibly be the meaning of the familiar liturgical words: "O Lamb of God, who takes away the sins of the world, have mercy on us"? Only Jewish people familiar with their own worship traditions would understand.

In the Jewish worship life the first symbol of Yom Kippur, the Day of Atonement, was the sacrificial lamb, which was said to have been offered for the sins of the people. The second symbol of Yom Kippur was a goat who was thought, quite literally, to be able to carry the sins of the people into the wilderness on its back. Both of these Yom Kippur images can be found shaping the telling of the story of the cross.

The sacrificial lamb of Yom Kippur had to be chosen on the basis of its physical perfection. It had to be a male, since males were more highly valued than females. It had to be examined carefully. The chief priests were charged with the task of doing a scrupulous investigation. Scratches, bruises or broken bones would disqualify the animal for this ceremonial role. The people of Israel could come into the presence of God only by way of a perfect offering. The physical perfection of the lamb was the first step in ensuring that process.

The lamb, as a subhuman creature, was not thought capable of participating in human sin. The lamb had no capacity to make moral judgments, or to choose to do that which was evil. So, in this manner, moral perfection was added to the animal's physical perfection. So it was that through this perfect offering, a sinful people believed they could enter God's presence.

Almost instantly, it now appears, Jesus came to be seen as the new lamb of Yom Kippur. His death was interpreted to be the perfect offering by which a sinful humanity could enter God's presence. It was so perfect that no further sacrifice was thought to be required. Note how the Gospels portrayed his physical perfection. He was a young Jewish male in the prime of his life. None of his bones were broken, said the interpretive text (John 19:36), and psalms, which pointed to this perfection, were readily quoted (Psalms 22:17, 34:10). Moral perfection was also claimed for this Jesus. He came to be thought of as the sinless one: "Tempted in all things and yet without sin," it was said of him. The offering of the morally perfect, but subhuman lamb of the Jewish Yom Kippur, had been transformed into the offering of the morally perfect but fully human Jesus. The whole world, now it was said, despite its broken sinfulness, could come into the presence of God through the sacrificial offering of a physically perfect, morally perfect son of God. Whatever the Jesus experience was, it seemed to issue in a sense of forgiveness and wholeness, which was immediately inter-

preted in terms of the lamb of Yom Kippur, a familiar symbol of
the Jews.

The second feature of Yom Kippur was the liturgy of the goat
(Leviticus 16:16-22). Once again a kid goat, a healthy specimen,
was brought into the solemn assembly of the people on the Day of
Atonement. The people were encouraged, in that assembly, to
confess their sins and to purge themselves of their sinfulness by
having the high priest symbolically place their sins on to the body
of the goat. When the goat was fully laden with the sins of the
people, then the people would curse the evil sin-bearing goat and
call for its expulsion. Finally, the goat would be freed to be driven
from the assembly of the people into the wilderness, carrying the
people's sins with it. In this liturgical act people believed themselves to have been cleansed, purged and freed of all their sins.
That goat came to be called the scapegoat, who had taken away
the sins of the people.

Jesus in his death was also interpreted under this Yom Kippur
symbol of the scapegoat. The portrait drawn of Jesus surrounded
by a hostile mob calling for his death and vilifying him with their
curses was designed to enable this identification with the scapegoat to be understood by those familiar with Yom Kippur. Jesus,
like the scapegoat, was taken beyond the walls or the boundaries
of the people. Golgotha was outside the city walls. Through this
Jesus the sins of the people were carried away. In this manner yet
another Jewish symbol was interpretively wrapped around Jesus of
Nazareth.

When the Jews chose the two animals to be used in the Yom
Kippur ceremony, please note that one was to be slain and the
other was to be released so that it could bear away the people's
sins. I suspect that this Jewish tradition also shaped the biblical
account of the releasing of the prisoner, Barabbas. Jesus and Barab-

bas were the two symbols like the two animals of the Yom Kippur tradition. One was slain and the other was freed to escape into the wilderness. It is the name of Barabbas that makes this possibility so real for me. The name Barabbas is made up of two words: *Bar*, which means "son," and *Abba*, which means "Father" or "God." So *Barabbas* means literally "Son of God." So in the passion story there are two figures; both are the Son of God just like at Yom Kippur when two animals were used in the penitential rite. One was put to death, the other was banished. How profoundly rich the Gospel story becomes when it is allowed to be illumined with its Jewish context.

I go into these Jewish images in this much detail to illustrate the fact that the story of Jesus is not told even in the Gospels as objective history. Rather, before the creation of the Gospels, Jesus had already been interpreted by the worship symbols out of the Jewish world in which he lived. The symbols of the particular Jewish past actually shaped the details that were written into the story of his life. Jesus can never be understood unless one places him deeply into his own first-century Jewish heritage. It is that setting that enables us to separate the interpretation of Jesus from the experience of Jesus. It allows us today to reject the traditional interpretations and yet still to be driven to explore the experience. These are the facts that historians will understand even better than theologians.

Aron, a historian of note, begins his quest for insight into the lost years of Jesus by starting with the content present in the Gospel story. Then he uses that content as a doorway through which he can walk to enable him to explore dramatically the Jewish terrain that lies behind the Jesus narrative. When he discovers that terrain, he finds in it startling new meaning that serves to illumine the life of this Jesus.

Aron works from his available data to probe the patterns of Jewish home life in the first century, seeking thereby to ascertain something of the way in which Jesus was reared. He explores the necessity faced by every Jewish male to learn a trade. Jesus was a carpenter, said an almost offhand remark recorded in the Gospel of Mark (6:31). Mark was the first Gospel to be written and was the basis upon which both Matthew and Luke were constructed some ten to twenty-five years later. As the years passed, the divine and miraculous nature of this Jesus was clearly heightened. Jesus was increasingly identified by Matthew, for example, with the image of the Son of Man who came on the clouds of heaven. The clue in Matthew 1:23 is in the word Emmanuel, which meant that the heavenly God was eternally present. Jesus appears in Matthew 28 as a heavenly being. The fact that he might have been a laborer working with his hands as a carpenter became less and less an appealing image. So Matthew changed Mark's verse and turned Joseph, not Jesus, into being the carpenter (Matthew 13:55).

Jesus was called the Son of Mary in Mark (6:3). In time that reference was also viewed as somewhat pejorative. It was not proper in the first century to refer to a grown Jewish man as the son of a woman. Those words suggested that there might be something a bit improper about his paternity. (This point is powerfully developed in *The Illegitimacy of Jesus* by Jane Schaberg.) Mark also referred to Jesus' mother, Mary, on only two occasions, and both of them were negative. She was a woman who was embarrassed by her son's strange behavior. She went to "take him away" because he was "beside himself" (Mark 3:31-35, 6:1-6). Mark gave no evidence that he had ever heard of a supernatural birth story about Jesus. Yet once again we find that the passage of time expands the aura surrounding Jesus. Matthew was the first Gospel writer to suggest a miraculous nature to Jesus' birth (Matthew 1,2). This birth story was used to explain Jesus' adult behavior, which was appropriate only if one understood who he really was and what his role as Son of God was all about. Yet, even those original Matthean narratives of Jesus' birth were beautifully crafted midrashic stories that Matthew's Jewish readership would certainly understand, and would not even be tempted to literalize. The story of the virgin was based on a text in Isaiah (7:14). The star in the east came out of the Mishnah where a similar sign had been used to announce the birth of Abraham, the birth of Isaac and the birth of Moses. It also found scriptural lodging in the story of Balak and Balaam (Numbers 22-24). The narrative of the wise men was crafted on the basis of Isaiah 60 with a throwback to a visit of the Queen of Sheba to King Solomon, a fond memory in Jewish history, when another royal personage traveled to pay homage to another king of the Jews (I Kings 10). King Herod, who slew the Jewish male babies in Bethlehem at Jesus' birth, was based on the ancient story of the Pharaoh who slew the Jewish male babies in Egypt at the time of Moses' birth (Exodus 1:22, Matthew 2:16-18).

The style of writing employed by the Jewish people lent itself to this kind of interpretive nonliteral understanding. God's actions were timeless to the Jews. These eternal signs of God's favor were simply wrapped around particular figures in Jewish history to indicate that the Holy God was once more making the divine presence felt in their ongoing history. Aron develops these concepts beautifully.

Christians, long separated from their Jewish religious heritage, have been taught to think of the Lord's Prayer as "the prayer Jesus taught us to pray." But Aron shows how deeply even that prayer was shaped by the Kaddish tradition of the Jewish people. He explains in detail the role that the kosher dietary laws played in Jewish life and suggests how they had found a place in Jesus' understanding. He hints at how the Jewish liturgical year shaped the organization of the Gospel material. These were ideas brought to full fruition in the work of an English scholar named Michael Goulder some thirty years later and hopefully popularized to a larger audience in my last book, *Liberating the Gospels: Reading the Bible with Jewish Eyes*.

Once the Gospels are laid out against the background of the liturgical year of the Jews, a remarkable confluence is established. The message of John the Baptist reflects quite consciously the themes from the festival of Rosh Hashanah, on which occasion the John the Baptist story must surely have first been read, at least in the original plan of Mark's Gospel. The story in Luke of the woman who washed Jesus' feet at the home of Simon the Pharisee (Luke 7:36-50) was put into that strange location by the Third Gospel because Luke needed a story about being cleansed from sin to be read as his lesson for Yom Kippur. (In both Mark 14:3-9 and Matthew 26:6-13 this story is located in the last week of Jesus' earthly life and is part of the passion story. In Luke it is placed in the early Galilean phase of Jesus' ministry before the journey to Jerusalem.) The parable of the sower, with its four different kinds of soil and its four different missionary explanations, was the perfect story to help the early Christians celebrate the eight days of Tabernacles, or Succot, the harvest celebration of the Jews, and so it found its place in Mark (4:1-20), Matthew (13:1-23) and Luke (8:4-15) at exactly the point when Tabernacles was being celebrated in the Jewish liturgical cycle. The story of Jesus' transfiguration (Mark 9:28, Matthew 17:1-8, Luke 9:28-36) was placed exactly at the point in the structure of the Gospels to enable it to be read against the background of the Jewish Festival of Dedication, which, for the Jews, celebrated the time when the light of God (the Shekinah) was restored to the Temple. How better could Christians assert that in Jesus a new meeting place, other than the

Temple, had been established between God and human life. As the light of God always had descended on the Temple in the past, now it was pictured as descending on Jesus as the new Temple. When the Temple was destroyed by the Romans in 70 C.E., this image became even more powerful. The last Gospel to be written quotes Jesus as saying, "Destroy this Temple and in three days, I will raise it up" (John 2:19). They did not understand, explained the Fourth Gospel, that he was referring to "the Temple of his body" (John 2:21). The earliest Jews, however, would have understood the symbol employed here.

We have already noted how the passion story of Jesus was related to the Passover celebration of the Jews. To complete the cycle of Jewish holy days, Shavuot or Pentecost, which marked the time God gave the Torah to the Jews at Mt. Sinai, surely shaped Matthew's version of the Sermon on the Mount, which was placed into Matthew's text to coincide with that celebration. The Sermon on the Mount, which is only in Matthew, was modeled after Psalm 119, which was the Psalm of Pentecost among the Jews. The Sermon on the Mount also contrasts the law of Moses with the new interpretation of the law given by Jesus. It was a perfect lection to be read in eight segments over the twenty-four hours in which the Jews observed a vigil as they celebrated their Festival of Pentecost.

Luke, who wrote his Gospel to speak to a more hellenized and less rigidly Jewish community of believers, did not follow Matthew's lead for his Pentecost lesson. He rather told as his Pentecost narrative a story that contrasted the Torah, God's great gift to the Jews, with the Holy Spirit, God's great gift to the people of the New Covenant. "I baptize with water," he had John the Baptist say, "but he will baptize you with the Holy Spirit and with fire" (Luke 3:14-22). Luke returned to this story when he wrote the second volume of his story, which we call the Acts of the Apostles. There he stated quite overtly, "When the day of Pentecost had come" (Acts 2:1) and then he proceeded to tell the story of the coming of the Holy Spirit and fire. Clearly the shaping presence of the Jewish liturgical year was still present in his narrative. The Gospels are more self-consciously Jewish books than most Christians have ever imagined. This is the point Robert Aron stresses in his own way again and again.

In the Gospel story we meet a rich cast of characters, which includes Pharisees, Sadducees and Zealots. Most of us read of them in that sacred text with little or no historical comprehension. Robert Aron gives us a thumbnail, but accurate, sketch of the history of the movement that produced the people who were marked by and included in these designations. His insights illumine the roles that Sadducees, Pharisees and Zealots played in the accounts of Matthew, Mark, Luke and John. We do not meet the Essenes in the Gospel texts, but they are in the Gospel story nonetheless, and Aron demonstrates just how the influence of the Essenes was present in the life of Jesus in a way few readers of the Gospels have ever imagined. Indeed, the possibility that Jesus himself was identified with the Essenes cannot be dismissed.

Aron also looks into certain unique features of Jewish worship that have also almost unconsciously shaped the Gospel tradition. The use of a plural pronoun "our" in prayer is a case in point. The plural pronoun revealed the corporate nature of the Jewish approach to God, as in "Our Father." The typically Jewish habit of quoting one authority after another in debates about the meaning of scripture, which helped the midrashic tradition to grow into volumes and volumes of commentary, is the insight against which Aron demonstrates the striking contrast that Jesus presented. It was startling indeed, inside this tradition, to hear Jesus quoted as saying,

"You have heard it said of old . . . but I say unto you." No wonder people said that he spoke as one having authority, and not as the scribes (Mark 1:22, Matthew 7:29, Luke 4:32).

Many other insightful references will greet the reader of this book, who will find Aron's work to be an illuminating pleasure. This book will also contribute mightily to the new awakening that marks the contemporary religious debate about just who this person Jesus of Nazareth really was and is. He was first and foremost a Jewish man of the first century who emerged out of that region we have called the Holy Land. But underneath all the images of his particular time and place, he was also one in whom the eyes of faith perceived "a God presence." That was the experience that required an explanation. His was a life through which transcendence seemed to invade human history. He was a means through which people came to believe that God had been revealed. This was a life into which people in every generation since have been invited to enter if in some way they wanted to touch that divine sense of eternity.

Robert Aron helps interpreters of the Gospels ask the appropriate question of those sacred texts. That question is not, "Did this episode literally occur?" That is a question posed by western Gentiles who have tried to objectify history and who understand nothing of the Jewish way of processing holy moments. That question will result in either a "yes" answer that will lead to an absurd literalism or a "no" answer that will lead to a vapid and empty liberal dismissal of the Jesus experience. The Jewish question is, "What does it mean?" What caused the Jewish interpreter to process whatever the Jesus experience was by wrapping Jesus inside the sacred history of the Jewish people. That is why there are in the Jesus story echoes of every episode in the Jewish past in which God had been perceived to have been present in human history. So in Jewish eyes Jesus became the new Joseph, the new Moses, the new Samuel, the new David, the new Solomon, the new Elijah, the new Elisha, the new Servant of Isaiah, the new Son of Man of Daniel. Yes, these and many more.

By probing the "lost years" of Jesus, not for legendary biographical adventures, but for solid edifying insights into the shaping culture and history of first century Galilee and Judea, Robert Aron has opened a significant door of understanding through which skeptics and believers alike might enter to reassess the power and the wonder, to say nothing of the legends and the mystique, that have surrounded Jesus of Nazareth.

I commend his seminal work to another generation.

Preface

A mystery between two mysteries. A mystery apparently human between two mysteries divine. Jesus' hidden years.

The hidden years of Jesus' life, those that the Gospels leave almost completely in the shadows, run from his return from Bethlehem to Nazareth, in earliest childhood, to his baptism by Saint John the Baptist, at the start of his preaching. They represent a period of his life marked by none of the supernatural signs that the Gospels tell us were attendant upon it both before and after. Jewish writers, attached to their own beliefs and respectful of those of Christians, may study these years without feeling indiscreet and at the same time without denying personal tradition. However formidable may be the difficulties of such a study, encouragement from two separate quarters has made the risk seem worth taking.

First that of Christian theologians, both Catholic and Protestant, who by their admission that Jesus had a double nature, human and divine, implicitly authorize the writer to deal with his human side alone. Among them, Saint Cyril of Alexandria declares: "The Wise Evangelist, having shown us the Word made Flesh, goes on to demonstrate that . . . he complied with the laws of the nature which he had made his own." And John Calvin: "Unless we wish to deny that Christ was made a real man we must not be ashamed to confess that he voluntarily submitted to all those things which cannot be separated from human nature."

Thoroughgoing Christians may find this book incomplete. But in spite of its self-imposed limitations it may have something to teach them.

Nine-tenths of the life of the being who for two thousand years has been the focus of hundreds of millions of people's religious aspiration are totally unknown. The mystery of the Nativity has for centuries been told over and over; the mysteries of the Passion and the Resurrection are familiar to both believers and unbelievers, but the thirty years between, the years of childhood, adolescence and maturity, so crucial in any human life, may as well never have existed.

The lives of Pontius Pilate and Herod, who endure simply because they were his contemporaries, are well documented, and those of Mohammed, Calvin and Voltaire, who respectively rivaled, reformed and denied his Church, are amply known. But the life of Jesus between the ages of one and thirty hangs on a few lines from one of the Gospels and a minimum of commentaries upon them.

The Gospel according to Luke, after telling us that the newborn babe was taken by his mother and Joseph from Bethlehem back to Nazareth, reveals in twelve words that he went through the normal physical and mental stages of a child's development: "The child grew and became strong, filled with wisdom. . . ." At twelve years of age this progress is confirmed: "and the favor of God was upon him."

It is at this time, in the verses immediately preceding this one, that we have the only known episode of Jesus' childhood.

> *Now every year his parents went to Jerusalem for the festival of the Passover.*
>
> *And when he was twelve years old, they went up as usual for the festival.*
>
> *When the festival was ended and they started to return, the boy Jesus stayed behind in Jerusalem, but his parents did not know it.*
>
> *Assuming that he was in the group of travelers, they went a day's journey. Then they started to look for him among their relatives and friends.*
>
> *When they did not find him, they returned to Jerusalem to search for him.*
>
> *After three days they found him in the temple, sitting among the teachers, listening to them and asking them questions.*
>
> *And all who heard him were amazed at his understanding and his answers.*
>
> *When his parents saw him they were astonished; and his mother said to him, "Child, why have you treated us like this? Look, your father and I have been searching for you in great anxiety."*
>
> *He said to them, "Why were you searching for me? Did you not know that I must be in my Father's house?"*
>
> *But they did not understand what he said to them.*
>
> *Then he went down with them and came to Nazareth, and was obedient to them. His mother treasured all these things in her heart.*

The above are the only references in the Gospels to the hidden years.

In the liturgy of the Passion, in the office for Good Friday, the sixth-century hymn by Venantius Fortunatus says in two lines:

Lustra sex qui iam peregit,
Tempus implens corporis . . .
Thirty years he dwelt among us,
His appointed time fulfilled . . .

Blaise Pascal, the 17th-century French philosopher, treats them in the single sentence: "Of his thirty-three years he lived thirty without making himself known."

The apocryphal Gospels, which do contain some lore of the early years, add meager information to the New Testament story.

Such a paucity of facts might well discourage biographical treatment. But it need not block the aim of this book, which is to retrace a spiritual journey.

If the thirty all-important years in which Jesus prepared his preaching mission are so obscure, perhaps it is because they were spent among the Jews. The purest Jewish thought, such as we find it in the Old Testament and the Talmud, makes little of facts unless they have some religious or spiritual significance. The day-to-day life of a person, no matter how great he or she may be, is of no interest except at the moments when it manifests God's will.

In the case of Moses, for instance, the Bible dwells at length upon the fateful circumstances of his birth, but there follows a long blank, interrupted by one isolated episode, until his life became one with that of the chosen people. The New Testament seems to deal with Jesus the same way. The Jews became interested in Jesus only after he had met with John the Baptist, for someone's personal life had little to do with sacred history except when it served to manifest the workings of God.

Hence the silence of first-century Jews about Jesus' hidden years. In their eyes this period did not seem to have sufficient importance in God's eye to merit survival. But in the disorder of today it may have a message for us.

One would like to venture far back into the past of Israel, to rediscover, perhaps, at certain points, the purity and innocence of ancient ceremonies in which the Jews have participated for thousands of years; those perhaps at which the philosopher Maimonides (A.D. 1135–1204) assisted, or the French Rabbi Rashi (A.D. 1040–1105), or even the early teacher Hillel (70 B.C.–A.D. 10), and those in which Jesus took part. The years during which Jesus attended these ceremonies, the years when he lived "without being known," these are the hidden years.

Two thousand years ago, in a part of Palestine where the religion of Israel had conserved its purity, a Jewish child was born. This book is not an attempt to recover irreparably lost facts, but rather to sift historical and spiritual influences. It has three purposes: first, to remind Jews of certain features of their religion; second, to give Christians a feeling for their religious origins; and third, by pointing up the conflict between the Jewish and pagan worlds of Jesus' day to illuminate the conflict between contemporary Christianity and a new paganism, a conflict that cannot be won unless we draw, discerningly, upon the sacred heritage that underlay Jesus' upbringing.

PART ONE
Before Jerusalem

CHAPTER ONE

The Return to Nazareth

WHEN JESUS' PARENTS BEGAN the three-day caravan trek from Nazareth to Bethlehem just before his birth, there were two reasons for the epic journey.

According to the Gospel of Matthew, it was in order to fulfill the Old Testament's prophecy of the Messiah's birthplace:

And you Bethlehem, in the land of Judah, are by no means the least among the rulers of Judah; for from you shall come a ruler who is to shepherd my people Israel.

Their journey was also a consequence of the Roman occupation of Palestine. The Jews, like all peoples of the Middle East, remained attached to the place of origin of their tribe or family, to their father's house (*bet abot*). The father's house might be broken up and the members of the family scattered, but they maintained tradition wherever they went.

The census of the population of Palestine, ordered by the Roman governor of Syria, Quirinus, just at the time of Jesus' birth, was anything but agreeable to the Jews. What "occupied" nation would not be apprehensive of any such measure imposed by the "occupying forces" upon it? In the case of the Jews, faithful to a religion they considered superior to that of their idolatrous conquerors, there was not only apprehension but also a strong will to "resist." The Romans, on their side, were skilled politicians. In order to obtain as large a measure as possible of "collaboration," they concentrated on the end rather than the means; the census must be taken, but they did not insist that it be at the actual place of residence, in the Roman manner. The Jews were left free to follow their own custom of grouping themselves according to their place of origin. And so Joseph chose to present himself at Bethlehem, which as a descendant of David (Luke 2:4) he considered his family home.

The journey to Bethlehem, broken by overnight stays at the house of a friend or a public stopping place, could not have taken less than three or four days. In view of the circumstances under which it was made, we may say that the child Jesus began his life under the double aegis of loyal obedience to Jewish tradition and of opposition to the customs imposed by pagan rule.

Nazareth, to which Joseph brought back Mary and Jesus, supposedly two years later, was a small village, lively or somber, according to the contemporary historian's retrospective point of view. For some historians, ancient Nazareth, overlooking the Esdrelon Valley from what is now the eastern part of the city, was neither important nor attractive. The unevenness of the terrain may seem picturesque to a present-day visitor, but to the biblical inhabitants it was doubtless only an inconvenience. Caves, dug out of the side of a hill, served to store food and also as dwelling places.

A spring, known today as the Virgin's Fountain, supplied water to the local people, as well as to caravans from the desert. All around there are low hills, and a thirty-foot cliff near the presumed site of the ancient synagogue. A mile and a half away a mountain, called Djebel el Qafse, rises nine hundred feet above the river. The natural attractions are few; Nazareth had hardly any share of the beauties of Canaan.

Other historians hold a different view. This village, which is mentioned in no ancient writings, not even the Talmud, and barely named as the subject of a third-century complaint, seems to them extremely agreeable. In the hills were whitewashed, mud-walled farmhouses, cypresses and olive groves, vineyards and wheat fields. Nazarenes tended gardens filled with lilies, verbena, and bougain-villeas.

However this may be, modern travelers cannot but be struck at first sight by the majesty of the scene. They find Nazareth built on a balcony of hills overlooking the plain that was formerly a highway for foreign invaders and often a battleground. And yet these gentle slopes and ravines, these huddled houses are far from the turbulent mainstream of history. One can imagine that this is a country of the soul, a natural site for some sort of religious evolution.

Whether or not Nazareth is physically a part of Canaan, it is spiritually close to this Promised Land, important even in prebiblical days for its contributions to the birth of more than one religion. For from time immemorial Canaan had a predestined sacred character. Everything combined to prepare it for this role, even the configuration of its rivers and valleys. Never, even in prehistoric days, was Canaan a flooded plain, like the Nile valley; its only hope of irrigation was in water from above. The earliest inhabitants' invocations to the heavens reflected their absolute dependence upon rain. In this way was born the adoration of transcendent divinities, which may be considered the prototype of the worship of today. As the *midrash*, or rabbinical commentary, of Ecclesiastes tells us: "Earth can be fertilized only by waters from on high, and so men raise their eyes to heaven and realize that they are dependent upon it."

Both geographically and climatically Canaan seems made for religious experience. Canaanites looked for the divine in the unpredictability and destructiveness of nature rather than in its beneficence.

Storms, floods and earthquakes, no matter how infrequent, haunt the conscience of primitive peoples. They come to the conclusion that God is not a tutelary spirit, peacefully sharing with them the benefits of heaven. God is kindly, to be sure, but God knows how to lighten and thunder, and does not calm the storm, or stop war or even prevent accidents. God has not taken on, as in our day, the aspect of an indulgent protector of those who choose to believe in a transcendent power. Becoming a part of history, staying at humankind's side, making no attempt to prevent the rumble of the thunder, the inundation of fields and cities, the destruction wrought by plague, war and death, God seems to suggest that all these accidents belong to a divine plan and have to do with salvation.

This dramatic sense of God, or of the gods and genies whose multiplicity led to this uniqueness, this perpetual debate between the land of Palestine and a sky from which humans expected everything, left its imprint not only on a succession of peoples— the Phoenicians, the Canaanites, the Hebrews—but also on the very soil, impregnated by the divine and marked with the traces of vanished forms of adoration and abolished sacrifices. Every mountain, river, spring, tree, cave and even stone calls up the presence of a deity or that of the prayers addressed to it. The excavation of prehistoric sanctuaries has revealed all sorts of traces; at Gezer, for instance, eight great stones in a row, some of them roughly squared, the others rounded, ranging from six to ten feet in height. What prayers and sacrifices, we wonder, did they receive? The top of one of them seems to be worn and polished by "the kisses, caresses and anointments of generations of the faithful." In the Negev desert, around Beersheba, and on the coast, near Ashkelon, archaeologists have found the superimposed layers of successive civilizations, from Neolithic days to our own. Within the range of our immediate interest, the Philistines, the Hebrews, the Greeks, the Romans and the Crusaders have trod this ground, leaving the altar of one religion upon another.

Stone, which survives its builder, has always been a vehicle of devotion. But in this religious reliquary, there are also remains of human sacrifices, which bear witness to the drama, the frenzy and the suffering that went with the apparition of divinity. There are urns containing the skeletons of babies no more than a week old, apparently stuffed into them alive and covered with sand, which has preserved them far longer than if they had enjoyed a normal life and received conventional burial. In the remains of a wall of the same sanctuary there is, alongside the babies the skeleton of a rheumatic old woman. Were the gods persuaded to be content with a less tender offering, or did a mother or grandmother choose to be buried alive beside the baby she had rocked on her knees?

Such things defy explanation; they must remain among the many secrets of the Holy Land. But one thing we know for certain: this land, consecrated from the beginning to the most rudimentary forms of religion, became the seat of the most important of all metamorphoses of the religious spirit, of which Israel was the agent.

We have had a glimpse of its polydemonic period, of the multiplication of genies and familiar spirits. Among the Canaanites, who preceded the Hebrews, there was worship of Astartes and Baals. And what were Baals? They were numberless local divinities, worshiped on high hills and under green trees. For there was not a single clod of earth or a single plant root through which the divine did not circulate, infinitely varied in shape and substance, with its only unity in the superstitious respect accorded to it by human worshipers. Each such divinity bore the name of Baal, accompanied by a sort of surname derived from the nature of the sacred object (mountain, tree or spring) or the place where it was located. Thus there was Baal Lebanon, the lord of Lebanon; Baal Tamar, the spirit of the palm tree; Baalat Beer, the lady of the well; Baal Perazim, the lord of the openings, that is, the wells; Baalat Gebal and Baal Gebal, lady and lord of Byblos . . . Other divinities owed their name not to the place where they lived, but to the power attributed to them: Baal Marqod, lord of the dance; Baal Berit, god of oaths and pledges; Baal Marpe, the healer; Baal Gad, master of happiness; Baal Zebub (Beelzebub), lord of the flies.

The sedentary Canaanites counted on all these Baals to fertilize their soil, to assure the fecundity of their herds, to guarantee their health and happiness. In our day all this may seem naive and superstitious. But these deities made for a sanctification of the world around human beings, a first religious fact of whose consequences we have not yet seen the end, and which may even arouse us to nostalgia. From this time to that of Jesus, Palestine became more and more divine, more and more human; supernatural manifestations multiplied, in response to the increasing fears and needs and hopes of men and women. Such a permeation with divinity was the outstanding attribute of this land, destined to be the source of good tidings and the scene of religious wars.

The good tidings, in the course of the centuries, assumed a variety of forms and of words to describe them. After the polydemonism of the Baals, submerged in matter, came the polytheism of gods whose earthly attachments were less local, so that they exercised a wider empire and had a function less subordinated to particular circumstances. The Canaanites adored Dagon, god of wheat and inventor of the plow; Shamash, the sun god, who gave light to humans; Adad, the god of the storm, who thundered where he pleased. The name of the city of Jericho is derived from the word *Yareah,* moon, which suggests the existence of a moon deity. Reshep, the god of fire; Barak, the god of lightning; Gad, the god of fortune, whose cult persisted clandestinely even in the age of monotheism and who was perhaps also a god of death, antedating the Hebrews' Yahweh and constituting a bridge to him—all these made up the polytheistic hierarchy, whose distinct and classified functions set it apart from the indiscriminate mass of demons and Baals that went before.

With its dedication to the divine on a broader and more orderly basis, with gods at the same time less numerous and more powerful, Palestine was still an essentially sanctified land, sanctified in its mountains and streams, its trees and dwellings. Only the formula of its sanctification was changed and perfected.

It was then that Israel came, that after the Canaanites the Hebrews reached the land promised to the first patriarch, Abraham, and his descendants, and proceeded to bring about a religious revolution. To them the question was simple, or so it seems to us, three thousand two hundred years after they resolved it. This land, consecrated by others but now theirs, was not to be stripped of a single one of its religious attributes; not the sparsest of its groves, the driest of its deserts or the barest of its mountaintops was to be profaned. But its total sanctification was to proceed not from a multitude of gods, but from the one God of the Hebrews. A new form of worship came into being, the outstanding Jewish contribu-

tion to religion, in which as many prayers and blessings were show-
ered upon the one God as had been directed to a multiplicity of
gods before. A blessing upon every act, a prayer for every eventual-
ity, an invocation with which to face every show of nature's power.
Hebrews prayed when they heard a clap of thunder, but not to a
thunder god; they blessed the fruit of the vine, but there was no
bacchic deity. They prayed in spots where their predecessors had
prayed, but not to the local genies who were supposed to inhabit
these locales.

Religion was a constant, but the nature of the communication
with divinity varied with the passage from one age to another.
Polytheism, with its specialized gods and rudimentary prayers, gave
way to monolatry and monotheism, with their omnipresent God
and diversified prayers. Monolatry was Israel's tribal worship of a
single God (which left room for other peoples to have gods of their
own); monotheism the transformation of Israel's God into the God
of all humankind. All through these changing phases the land bore
the same harvest of prayers, always abundant, but differently divided.

Throughout its prehistory and history, all the way to Jesus'
return to Nazareth, at the beginning of his formative years, Palestine had the same vocation. Amid the mobility of its winds and
waters and the permanence of its earth and stone, this was the land
where human met God and God met human. A land where nothing was profane, because nothing was inanimate or inhuman, a
land destined to revelations. Nazareth was a village marked by this
destiny and peculiarly suited to be the site of a new episode of its
fulfillment.

Palestine was not the only seat of Jewry at this time; its half-
million inhabitants were only one-tenth of those who lived in
Egypt and Greece and other profane lands. And Nazareth was
hardly a dot on the map, numbering no more than a few hundred

lowly people. It was an out of the way, self-sufficient place; up until the fourth century A.D., although the rest of the country was very much "occupied," it seems to have suffered no infiltration of Greeks or Romans. The inhabitants were simple, peasants and rustic artisans, patriotic in the narrowest sense of the word, at least according to the more sophisticated townspeople, who spoke Greek and Latin. Their uncouth pronunciation of Aramaic, the common language of the time, caused them to be held up to ridicule. "Can there any good thing come out of Nazareth?" said Nathaniel in the Gospel according to John, just as Montesquieu asked: "How can anyone be a Persian?" The Nazarenes were contemptuously called *am ha-aretz*, men of the land. But the land of Palestine, the Eretz Israel, is impregnated with the presence of God. So that this sarcastic nickname was actually creditable to the Nazarenes; it defined their mission.

In returning to Nazareth the holy family was governed by the same principles that had determined its departure for Bethlehem: respect for Jewish tradition, which was particularly strong in this simple, isolated place; resistance to the Roman invaders, who had no hold upon it; and, of course, obedience to God, whose presence seemed so near in these surroundings. Jesus' return to Nazareth coincided with a period when the doors of the temple of Janus in Rome were closed, because there was no war. But we know, to our cost, that the absence of war is not always peace.

Palestine's relation to Rome was that of what we call a "satellite." Herod was king, but although he was born on Jewish soil he was not of predominantly Jewish blood. His mother, Cypros, was Arabian; his father, Antipater, an Idumaean, and neither of them of royal birth, so that Flavius Josephus describes him as "from a house of common people." His kingship was due neither to his adopted country nor to the will of his compatriots: he had sought and brought it back from Rome. Flavius Josephus, himself a renegade Jew and hence sympathetic toward him, describes not without admiration the circumstances of his investiture:

> *Messala and Atratinus after him convened the Senate, and presenting Herod, dwelt on the good deeds of his father . . . Antony came forward and informed them that it was also an advantage in their war with the Parthians that Herod should be king. And as this proposal was acceptable to all, they voted accordingly . . . Now when the Senate was adjourned Antony and Caesar went out with Herod between them, and the consuls and other magistrates leading the way, in order to sacrifice and to deposit the decree in the Capitol. Then Antony entertained him on the first day of his reign . . .*

Such was the crowning of a collaborationist king. Herod won this reward by the extraordinary vigor with which, as governor of Galilee, he had pursued the "brigands," who may really have been political rebels. At his orders their chief, Ezekias, and a number of others were executed without trial, in violation of the Jewish law that safeguards the accused and considers them innocent until they have been found guilty.

Before the Jewish Sanhedrin, called together to judge his impropriety, Herod did not present himself as custom demanded, "humble . . . fearful . . . letting his hair grow long and wearing a black garment," but clad in purple and surrounded by armed soldiers. The judges were afraid; only one among them, Sameas, roused their sense of justice. They were about to condemn him when the high priest, Hyrcanus, put the sentence off until the next day and during the night helped Herod to get away. An unconventional disposal of the case, which Herod did not repay with gratitude, since later on, after he became king, he had the whole lot of his former judges, except Sameas, killed.

Herod remained faithful to Rome, and to whatever party seemed most likely to be in power. When Augustus overcame Antony, his benefactor, the King of Judea shifted his allegiance without the least loss of aplomb. Having paved the way for the changeover by sending troops to help Augustus' lieutenant, Ventidius, against Antony's gladiators, Herod went to see Augustus himself at Rhodes. Flavius Josephus tells us that he had laid aside his crown but not his dignity and that he boldly admitted having previously sent Antony money and supplies even if he had not fought at his side.

> *I have not deserted him upon his defeat at Actium . . . but have preserved myself, though not as a valuable fellow soldier, yet certainly as a faithful counselor, when I demonstrated to him that the only way he had to save himself and not lose all his authority was to slay Cleopatra . . . None of such advices would he attend to, but preferred his own rash resolutions before them, which have happened unprofitably for him but profitably for you . . . There is no room for me to deny what I have done . . . but if you will put him out of the case, and only examine how I behave myself to my benefactors in general and what sort of friend I am, you will find by experience that I shall do and be the same to myself.*

No Greek or Roman historian is a model of exactitude. But under Flavius Josephus' rhetoric we can easily detect the gross wiles with which Herod sought to win over his new master. He brings out the fact that he had never fought against him with his own hands, he condemns the blind passion of his conquered enemy, wishes death to Cleopatra and finally swears fidelity. By putting forward his own "virtue," Herod contrived to keep a post in which he could continue to levy his exactions.

For Herod was a pitiless and depraved man. Although he called himself a Jew his court was given over to pagan excesses—adultery, incest and even sodomy—to cruelty in all its forms and to a display of luxury that was in painful contrast to the poverty of the subjected people.

In 29 B.C. he killed his Hasmonean wife, Mariamne. A few months later, he ordered the death of his mother-in-law, Alexandra. Two of the children born to him by his wife, whom he claimed to love for her sake, were sent to Rome and hospitably received by Augustus, but as soon as they returned to Jerusalem he had them put to death, in spite of Augustus' efforts to save them. Sadistic and perhaps abnormal in other ways as well, such was the nature of the "friend and ally of Rome" who ruled over Palestine. Like many others of his kind, he had recourse to honeyed words and deception. One day, the Talmud tells us, he went anonymously to see a rabbi and tried to induce him to speak against the government. But the rabbi, suspecting a trap, answered him with a verse from Ecclesiastes: "Curse not the king, no not in thought . . . for a bird of the air shall carry the voice, and that which has wings shall tell the matter."

An understandably prudent reply, for this king, so anxious to know his subjects' opinions, had set up a network of secret police to ferret them out. He was also a man whose actions were contrary to his promises. Ostensibly he respected and encouraged the Jewish religion, in accord with his Roman masters—did not Augustus contribute personally to the support of the Temple at Jerusalem?—but at night he was known to have forced his way into the tomb of David and robbed it for its treasures.

The people knew little of the details of government or of the exact nature of the ties between Palestine and the Roman Empire. But ignorant as they were of politics, a king was a king, and they heard talk about him. Rumor, which in Semitic countries is so quick to spread and so easily distorted, held Herod responsible for

all the griefs of the Jewish country people, including those of
Nazareth. Poverty, heavy taxes and the petty annoyances imposed
by the bureaucracy and the police, all these things were blamed no
more on the Romans than on their royal collaborator. Doubtless
no one in Nazareth had ever seen him in person. But his name
served as a personification (a device particularly necessary to the
Semites) of evil.

The Nazareth to which Jesus and his family returned possessed
nothing remotely resembling a theological school or a political
institution. Religion, naively tied to the sanctified land, was the
most powerful force, and the only outside news was that brought
by the "bird of the air," in other words by rumor. What a contrast
between these two factors of everyday life; the one a product of
the land's natural evolution, the other imposed by a foreign power
to which the puppet king was subservient!

A tradition, an invasion—there was a mutual play of influences
between them. Herod, the incarnation of evil, was not merely a
commonplace tyrant; he was the servant of idolaters whose overwhelming material power was imposed upon a nation dedicated to
the one true God.

And so Palestine's struggle to escape from the Roman yoke can
be considered from two angles. It could have been political and
military, as the Zealots (forerunners of the "underground") conceived it, or spiritual and pacifist (relying on ideas rather than
weapons), as exemplified in the Pharisees.

When Jesus returned to Nazareth he was only a small child, far
from the age when he must make a choice between them. And
Joseph, the head of the family, was more anxious to get on with his
carpentry business than to concern himself with politics. It was by
making yokes and plowshares that he could best serve God. But in
the course of the hidden years, Jesus must have had to face the

problems of his country and of his times, problems common to many later countries and times as well. As a small child, in A.D. 6 he may have heard of the revolt of Judas of Gamala, known as the "Galilean," which caused considerable commotion before the Romans finally put it down. He had, during his first twelve years, to learn to feel like a Jew, to understand all the implications of Judaism. And when he went, at twelve years of age, to Jerusalem, it was not only, as the Gospel according to Luke tells us, to meet the doctors, but also to make his first contact with the power of Rome and the Jews who supported it. This was doubtless a decisive moment of his spiritual development.

A tradition, an invasion . . . that is, a land historically impregnated by God, and a group of men from another country who temporarily occupied it. From their meeting, and its effect on the mind of a predestined Jewish child, came the gravest crisis—still unresolved—through which humanity has ever passed.

Two years after Jesus' birth, at about the time when he returned to Nazareth, the seventy-year-old Herod the Great, loaded with wealth and honors, died.

CHAPTER TWO

Learning a Language and a Trade

Up to Jesus' thirteenth year we know almost nothing, at least officially, about him. But there is room for conjecture. We know nothing of his joys and sorrows, his childhood diseases and the other petty events of his early years. The little we do know concerns his professional apprenticeship.

For Joseph, who was by family tradition a carpenter, initiated him to the same trade. This was not simply on account of a parent's natural wish to assure his son's future and the satisfaction of seeing him follow in his footsteps. There was a religious reason as well. To the Jews of the Bible and to all those who even today are faithful to their tradition, manual labor, and indeed all labor, is sacred. "He who works for a living is greater than he who shuts himself up in idle piety," say the rabbis. And even more precisely: "An artisan at his work does not need to defer to the greatest of doctors."

Even the rabbis were enjoined to work. "Master some trade outside your studies," says the rabbinical comment on Ecclesiastes, and the Talmud stresses the fact that work has a higher place than even religious practices. "He who makes himself useful by work is greater than he who knows God." And intellectual work is not what is intended. "The best work is that connected with the land," says the Talmud, "even if it is not the most profitable it is to be preferred to all others."

The wise men of Israel, both before and after Jesus, have carried out these commands. Hillel was a woodcutter, Rabbi Yehuda a baker, Rabbi Johanan a cobbler. Even Saul of Tarsus, before he became Saint Paul, was a tent maker.

But it is not enough to exercise a trade; a man must hand it down to his son. Here, too, the Talmud is unequivocal. "Just as it is necessary to feed one's son, so it is necessary to teach him a manual trade." And again, in stronger terms: "A man who does not teach his son a trade is making him into a thief."

We can see now why Joseph made Jesus his apprentice, doubtless at a very early age, and why, over a century later, Saint Justin affirmed that he had heard mention in Palestine of plows from Joseph's workshop, made by Jesus' hand. For the first twelve of the hidden years, before the journey to Jerusalem, this is the only fact we really know, although it does not appear in any of the Gospel stories.

Let us go on, now, to conjectures. If we know that a person was born in New York, Moscow, Paris or New Delhi, it is easy enough for us to guess the person's language, culture and even religion. For the child Jesus the same thing holds true. There are two consequences, apparently obvious and commonplace, of the fact that he was born a Jew: he spoke a Semitic language and he practiced the religion of Israel.

Jesus' mother tongue was Aramaic, a language different from Hebrew, but fairly close to it, which for three centuries had taken its place in Palestine. Hebrew and Aramaic were as close as, in our day, French and Italian. Just as these are both Latin languages, based on the same mental makeup, so Hebrew and Aramaic were two Semitic tongues, with the same relationship between words and ways of thinking and easily translatable one to the other.

Later on, as an adult, Jesus was to live in a trilingual society, not unlike that of North Africa today, where Moslem intellectuals, of Semitic origin, have Arabic as a literary language, Berber for everyday use, and French for cultural exchanges. Jesus was familiar with traditional Hebrew and everyday Aramaic and probably had a smattering of Greek and Latin, the latter the country's official tongue. When he was nailed to the cross a sign carrying inscriptions in Greek, Latin and Hebrew was placed over his head.

His immediate task, then, was to learn Aramaic, and we must not underestimate the influence of this Semitic language upon his mental processes. The first characteristic that must have impressed itself upon him was its repugnance to abstraction. Every Semitic word is tied to two concrete realities: the reality of the mouth that pronounces it and the reality of the object that it designates.

The syllables by which the child learned to read were different from those that would be set before him today. In a contemporary primer vowels and consonants are presented on the same footing, each with an equal role to play. Consonants direct and articulate the breath, but if they were alone they would be unpronounceable, either too guttural or too whistling, in either case too close to mere noise to be read aloud. Vowels provide pauses; they contribute intonation and serve to infuse with thought and to orchestrate the primitive themes of the voice.

But the scrolls of the Torah from which Jesus learned to read were a very different affair. When he went to the *bet ha-sefer*, or kindergarten of his day, there was no question of learning to read or write vowels; for as long as five or six centuries after his birth they were simply not written. Even the Tetragrammaton, the incommunicable, four-letter, sacred name of Yahweh, before which Jesus, like every Jewish child, covered his eyes with his hand, was composed of only consonants. But of course all Jews had heard the Torah long before they saw it, and its verses were familiar to them by ear rather than by eye. Their reading was guided by the framework of consonants, with the missing vowel sounds supplied by memory and tradition.

After syllables came words. These too were down-to-earth in such a way as to confirm the healthy ingenuousness of a child. There was a strict minimum of adjectives, which in more evolved languages weaken the noun. Such adjectives as there were expressed elementary qualities such as a child could grasp, because he saw them around him. Big (*gedol*), little (*katan*), heavy (*kaved*), wise (*hakam*), every child has seen objects or persons thus described in his family life and during his initiation to the outside world. More subtle concepts were expressed by complementary nouns, so that in every sentence the substantive was sovereign. Holy place was place of holiness; eternal home, home of eternity; royal race, race of royalty; merciful kings, kings of mercy. In all these expressions there is a certain primitive character, but for this very reason they sank deeply into the consciousness of a child growing up in a faraway time and place and made him directly aware of the nature of human thoughts and emotions.

There was a paucity, too, of degrees of comparison, of the comparatives and superlatives and also of adverbs, of all the parts of speech that so often make for verbal inflation. Why use a roundabout expression to designate the holiest part of the Temple of Jerusalem, when it can so succinctly and effectively be called *kedosh hakedoshim*, the Holy of Holies? Why speak of the best or most beautiful of songs instead of the Song of Songs? Was not Mary more touched by the Angel Gabriel's telling her that she was "blessed among women," than if he had called her the happiest woman on earth? There are overtones of Semitic simplicity even in the Greek of the Gospel according to Luke.

In any case, the vocabulary that Jesus learned at home or in the bet ha-sefer was stripped down to essentials, to the nouns that initiate an act and the verbs that accomplish it. The language is devoid of artificial subtleties and expressive of naive faith; indeed, it has been called the language of God and that of God's poets and prophets. There are two categories of persons to whom it is utterly unsuited: philosophers and technocrats, for it cannot be adapted to either dialectics or mathematical speculations.

Jesus' direct contact with Semitic patterns of thought caused him to understand effortlessly certain expressions that we, with our Latin heritage, have misinterpreted. Take, for instance, the famous law of retaliation: "An eye for an eye, and a tooth for a tooth," which shocks us because we have accepted it, literally, as meaning that evil should be returned with evil. This is, of course, an error, based on our ignorance of the peculiar qualities of the Semitic languages. First, retaliation is a legal, not a moral, measure. Second, the Jews of Jesus' time, and Jesus himself, recoiled from abstraction and had no legal vocabulary. We cannot imagine them leafing through a penal code in order to find a penalty, general or particular; such procedure is remote from the spirit of the parables. The fact is that the Jews spoke in concrete metaphors, of which this is one. "An eye for an eye" does not mean that a man who has torn out the eye of his fellow should have his own torn out in return; this would be contrary to the Jewish law of loving one's neighbor as one's self and having mercy on one's enemy. It is a typically Semitic metaphor, meaning that there is an appropriate punishment for every crime, the loss of an eye being certainly graver than that of a tooth. Here we have nothing pitiless. Is it not the custom in every civilized country to fit the punishment to the crime? With his Semitic background Jesus could not have found this so very shocking.

The Talmud, which, as we shall see later, was already in the process of formation in Jesus' time, gives a subtle and slightly ironical reply to Latinized commentators on the law of retaliation.

> *Rabbi Simeon ben Johai says: "An eye for an eye" refers to a pecuniary punishment, that is the payment of a sum of money equivalent to the damage done. And why not retaliation in the literal sense of the word, that is, the infliction of the same damage in return? Because this would lead to all sorts of inequity. If a one-eyed man were to tear out one eye of his fellow, then he would completely lose his sight in return. And what punishment are we to inflict on a blind man who is guilty of this same crime?*

This is a humorous and conclusive example of how not to interpret a Semitic metaphor. To Jesus its meaning would have been perfectly clear.

Another contemporary error, of which he would never have been the victim, is in the interpretation of the phrase "vanity of vanities," as modern languages have translated one of the opening verses of Ecclesiastes. How abstract is this translation! It becomes a philosopher or a theologian, and neither one existed in the Nazareth of Jesus' time.

The Hebrew term is different from its Latin equivalent; it is the very concrete noun *hevel*, which means wind, breath, steam, or vapor, so that *hevel havalim* signifies "vapor of or from vapors."

Here is the intimate and graphic explanation given by the *midrash,* which Joseph might have passed on to Mary and Jesus, on one of those afternoons of the Sabbath day, dedicated to meditation of the Scriptures.

> *The vapor which rises from a cauldron of boiling water is not "vapor of vapors"; it is the vapor of the liquid from which it is distilled. But let us imagine seven cauldrons, one on top of another, with only the bottom one full of water. The vapor rising from this bottom cauldron will progressively lose substance as it mounts from one level to another, until finally it seems to be held up by other gusts of vapors. Then, and then only, we may call it "vapor of vapors."*

Let us go on from here to interpret the metaphor by the traditional Jewish method. The farther that intangible, vaporous thing, conscience, travels away from the God that made it, the more prone it is to the feeling of futility and despair described by the author of Ecclesiastes.

In the house at Nazareth, where he acquired his first notions of the world and of God, Jesus must have learned through images and analogies of just this kind. To modern people, brought up on the rationalism of Aristotle and Descartes, such unabstract, down-to-earth reasoning seems on the one hand extraordinarily poetical and free, on the other bewildering and terrifying. Without our grammatical rules, our dialectical formulas, our geometrical logic, we are like snails without a shell. But the Jew of Jesus' time had no such feeling of insecurity. The simple, ingenuous world, to which Hebrew and Aramaic furnished him the key, had a coherent meaning all its own, different from ours, but no less valid. There was no hiatus between objects and words, no metaphysical anxiety brought on by a dissonance between them. If, at a distance of two thousand years, we can have any idea of the use to which Jesus put words, we must be struck by the certainties that they represented to him.

First, the name of God, or one of its equivalents, had a terrifying reality and power. God was aware of the import of the holy name and on guard against it. Here, according to the *midrash*, is God's reaction to the words used to designate God in place of the forbidden name: "If men have invoked my surname as a pretext for killing one another, how much more would they have killed had I revealed my ineffable name?"

What a realistic absence of illusions!

To the Jew of ancient times every proper name was divinely inspired. Before his disobedience Adam was granted the power of giving a name to every living thing, and Moses, upon his ascent to heaven, was supposed to find God weaving wreaths of letters. Names were anchored in reality; they were not, as in our day, merely convenient labels; rather, they expressed the essence of a person or place and determined a destiny. Thus John (Johanan) means "God is gracious"; Emmanuel means "God is with us"; and Jesus means "Savior." In the book of Genesis, every time a person is born we are told the meaning of his or her name.

Place names are equally meaningful. Bethany, a town near a place where a boat crossed the River Jordan, means "home of the boat"; the bare rocky height of Golgotha means "cranium"; the garden of Gethsemane an "oil press." Bethlehem originally owed its name to the Babylonian god, Lakhmu, but after the arrival of the Israelites its etymology underwent a change and it came to mean *Bet-lehem*, or "house of bread."

What security and assurance the harmony between persons and places and their names afforded a child! A universe without flaw or fissure, where reason could never go astray, was opened up before him or her.

Common nouns, too, had no abstract significance. In a more modern language, grammar and rhetoric define the shades of meaning attached to every word. But in a Semitic tongue what matters is the logical content, its power over people, the emotion it awakens and the atmosphere it creates around them. Ideas far removed from one another intellectually but closely allied on a sentimental plane may inhabit the same word.

Zaddik, the key word of the Jewish moral code, indicates both justice and charity and the inseparable union between them. *Shalom,* that eternal Jewish aspiration, signifies not only peace, but also happiness and perfection. This variety of meanings may seem to make for logical imprecision. But there are advantages of another kind in the network of affinities and suggestions that enrich a word and push it deep into the consciousness, where emotion plays a greater part than dictionary definition. A person's inner life is one with language; at the center of vocabulary, certitude and serenity are found.

Humans are at the center of the universe as well; even Hebrew syntax contributes to this impression. In Latin, for instance, there is a genitive case to indicate possession—*domus patois,* the father's house—in which the possessor rather than the object possessed is inflected. This is tantamount to considering the object the stable element of the two and the father the variable. In biblical Hebrew the exact opposite is true. The object involved undergoes a change of case because of being possessed by the father, and the possessor remains unvaried. The house (*bait*) of the father (*ab*) becomes *bet-ab.*

Latin scholars and those brought up on a Latin language are disturbed by this reversal of the genitive, which reflects a mental process diametrically opposite to our own. But if we try to imagine the makeup of first-century Jews we at once realize that there is nothing so startling about it. At the center of their language and their world was humankind. As a nineteenth-century Jewish thinker, Elie Benamozegh, puts it: "Man is universe made conscious." Was not such a feeling profoundly comforting to a young child?

The vocabulary that Jesus learned as a child was, then, very close to life; it took now a human, now a divine turn, but was never shut up in theoretical concepts. It may have been somewhat fuzzy at the edges, but this was because it had the elasticity of real life, which is not always rational.

Let us pass, now, from substantives to verbs, notoriously a difficult part of any language. The way they were conjugated in the age of Jesus was equally revealing of the Jewish spirit. First, the Semitic verbal system does not hinge on time. To a Westerner this may seem disconcerting, but to a Semite it is another means of feeling at ease in the universe. "To primitive man," says philosopher Lucien Lévy-Bruhl, "time is not, as it is to us, a sort of intellectualized intuition, an 'order of succession.' It is felt rather than plotted." The Talmud itself says that there is no before and no after.

In other words, time's value is not absolute; it depends upon the people who animate it. Time does not shut them in or obsess them, rather it holds them up, as a bird is held up by air and a fish by water. Both these elements flout first in one direction and then in another. Why, then, should time be a one-way street? Semitic verbs do not merely recount a fact or an action; they may also express an order, a prohibition or a condition such as doubt or desire. In grammatical terms a verb may be hortatory, optative and so on; rarely is it a plain indicative. All these are abstract ways of stating what Jesus instinctively felt, what the Jews of his time knew, if not in fact, then by intuition: that time can be measured only by the impulsion given it by people, that it has no fixed value outside their experience of it.

None of this is very Cartesian. The time we have been discussing is not the geometrical framework in which for two thousand years people have noted the stages of their technical progress
and their spiritual decline. For Jews of biblical times this humaniza-
tion of time was in harmony with a deep and intimate feeling that
may have weakened them in regard to the Romans but strengthened them in their own conscience and before God.

Let us look at the *midrashim*, or rabbinical commentaries, and
the Talmud whose accumulated wisdom and allegory surrounded
Jesus when he was a child. Here the chronology of the world
appears to have been foreordained by God and yet at the same time
dependent upon humans. Doubtless the all-knowing Creator knew
from the time of Genesis what would be the decisive moments of
the evolution of the universe and of the destiny of Israel, which
was its focus. But the dates of these events were subject to modification by human merits and faults. God had originally meant to
reveal the Torah, or Law, only to the thousandth generation after
the Creation, leaving humankind time to attain perfection on its
own initiative, to discover by its own experience the as-yet unfor-
mulated precepts of God's wisdom. But God's optimism soon
proved to be unfounded. Instead of seeking the revelation of the
Law, men seemed to be intent upon evading it. Adam disobeyed,
Cain killed, and the human race was corrupted, as in Sodom and
Gomorrah. Even the patriarchs, one *midrash* of the time of Jesus
tells us, were disappointing. Abraham doubted God's promises;
Isaac continued to love his son, Esau, whom God had condemned
for his violence, thus showing himself unfaithful to the Lord;
Jacob, according to the prophet Isaiah, accused God of failing to
reward his merits, which was tantamount to rebellion.

After such reprehensible behavior on the part of the best of
God's children, God feared that humankind would fall into further

corruption and chose to reveal the Law not to the thousandth but to the twenty-sixth generation. (There were ten generations between Adam and Noah, ten between Noah and Abraham and six between Abraham and Moses.) If the order of events in time can be thus influenced by people, why should not verb tenses also undergo alteration? This is what a young Jew learns from the study of the conjugations. In a Latin language we find present, future and past tenses, each of them referring to a well-defined segment of time. But the different viewpoint of Hebrew grammar is illustrated in two examples of words attributed to God in person.

First, there is the *midrash* account of God's revelation, through Moses, to the Children of Israel: "The Holy One, blessed be his name, said to Moses 'Tell them that I was, that I am and that I shall be.'" In the Hebrew, the three tenses are one, the imperfect; in the English of the King James Version, this is translated as a present: "I am that I am" (Exodus 3:15).

When after Moses' death, God confirmed the promises regarding the Children of Israel to Joshua, God used the tenses in an even more confusing way. "Every place that the sole of your foot will tread upon I have given to you, as I promised to Moses" (Joshua 1:3). In the Hebrew the first of the three verbs is an imperfect and the last two are perfects. To us the sequence of tenses is puzzling, but to Jesus and his contemporaries it was perfectly clear. The perfect and the imperfect do not refer to a definite moment of time, but to its movement. To the biblical Jew, and perhaps to the modern Arab as well, it does not matter at what moment an action took place, but only whether or not it has been accomplished. The Semitic languages demand of a verb only that it mark the difference between finished and unfinished business. The flow of time is what counts, not its successive stages. When God proclaimed a personal existence or renewed a promise to Joshua, God did not think in calendar

terms, but simply inscribed that existence in duration, on a basis of
relativity akin to that discovered by the Jewish-born philosopher
Henri Bergson. The Hebrew imperfect is applied to a continuing,
that is "open" action, the perfect to one that is finished and "closed."
In the verse from Joshua, the phrase "every place that the sole of
your foot shall tread upon" refers to an action that may be repeated
any number of times but never be finished; God's promise to
Moses and Joshua, on the other hand, was made once and forever.

By these and many other similar phrases the Jewish concept of
time was impressed upon Jesus' youthful mind. Even if he was
unable to put it into words he was instinctively aware of the difference between the finished and the unfinished. Of course we cannot follow the exact course of his mental development. First,
because he was Jesus, and his mission, whether we look on it as
human or divine, surpasses our understanding; second, because he
was a child and the origin of a child's thoughts are mysterious to
us, and third, because he was a Palestinian Jew whose mental
process had an empirical character different from our own.

But even if we cannot follow the development we can see the
end result. Jesus, along with the other Jews of his time, had an idea
of time that may still be found today in isolated Jewish communities. Until the nineteenth century the Ashkenazi Jews of Central
Europe retained the biblical concept of time. To them the present
moment knew no limits but was part of a continuum stretching
from the beginning to the end of time, that is, from the Creation
to the advent of the Messiah. Their life was not led on a chrono-
logical basis, for the patriarchs, kings and prophets of the Old
Testament were always at their side. They believed themselves to be
living in the past of Israel and at the same time in its future.

At the Passover feast, the Seder, which Jesus celebrated first
under its Jewish name and then as the Last Supper, all participants

present consider themselves as one of those freed from bondage in Egypt, as an incarnation of the past. At the same time they represent the future; there is a place left empty at the table for the prophet of the Messiah, Elijah.

The whole of Jewish worship is a reconstruction of history. On the feast of Purim, for instance, the children in the synagogue stamp their feet at the name of Haman, as if he were still alive or only just killed, and in so doing they think of all the persecutors still in the limbo of the future, waiting to play their role of murderers and then, like him, to perish. So it is that for a Jew every fleeting moment has something of the savor of eternity. Present, past and future run together, and in their meeting the present does not play a part of mere regret or expectation; it is, on the contrary, the link by which history is made to remain alive, by which the future is present before it has arrived and the past lives after it has gone by. There is a curious *midrash* concerning a certain Rabbi Lieber's vision of the prophet Elijah, which emphasizes the importance of the present. "It is not Rabbi Lieber who is privileged to have a revelation of Elijah, but Elijah who is privileged to have a revelation of Rabbi Lieber."

Among all the fugitive moments in which eternity dwells, the most organic, the most holy, is that of the consecrated rest of the Sabbath, or seventh day, which provides a framework for the Jewish notion of time. Abraham Heschel says:

> *Jewish tradition never defined the concept of eternity, but it does tell how to experience the taste of it on earth. Eternal life is within us, growing beyond us. The world to come is therefore not only a posthumous condition, dawning upon the soul on the morrow after its departure from the body. The essence of the world to come is Sabbath eternal, and the seventh day in time is an example of eternity.*

When syntax introduced into the Jewish makeup a distinction between the finished and the unfinished, there were serious cultural as well as religious consequences. From a religious point of view it showed that, for the Jews, time is almost sacred, or at least that it belongs to the sanctified universe of the Bible and of Jesus. Sacred because it is the crucible where God's eternity meets human temporality. Sacred also because, in its differentiation between the finished and the unfinished, there is the basis of Messianism—of the accomplishment, unaccomplished yet constantly sought, a concept that Israel was the first to make the motive power of human progress, and one that Jesus must have absorbed from his earliest years.

Culturally, this distinction is the basis for the clash between the Semitic and Roman worlds, in which Jesus, during the years of his ministry, played so large a part, in which he physically succumbed, only to win an eventual spiritual victory. This clash was not a purely political affair, between an empire and its satellite; it was the conflict between two cultures, two conceptions of life.

For the Romans and all those who have undergone their influence, "time is an instrument of measure rather than life's domain." But for Jesus and the Jews it is the very stuff of life, upon which people can embroider the pattern of their days. For the Romans and the technocrats who are their spiritual descendants, the purpose of culture is to conquer space and to subordinate time to spatial categories. But for Jesus and the Jews of his time, the purpose of all spiritual endeavor was to sanctify time. Abraham Heschel goes on:

> *People are so identified with time that they cannot detach themselves from it. The world of space is all around us, but it contains nothing so indispensable that we cannot do without it; in fact, we are quite free to change our spatial situation. Existence does not imply any spatial power, but to the years of our life we*

give overwhelming importance. Time is the only thing we really possess, and so naturally that unless we make an effort we are not aware of it. Our journey is in time, which flows like a mighty river, with familiar objects represented by the shore.

Such may have been the first impression that the Semitic world made upon the child Jesus' mind. It is likely that the Semitic idea of time had an important part in determining his spiritual progress. Indeed, it may have been a factor in the later antagonism between Jesus and the Romans and the Romanized Jews, their collaborators, who judged him at Jerusalem. This conflict between the Semitic and Roman worlds is the dramatic background out of which Christianity was born.

CHAPTER THREE

Jesus in the Synagogue

IN THE NAZARETH OF Jesus' time there were doubtless Jews both faithful and faithless. Israel, the nation chosen by God to incarnate God's will, has always been a people of priests and a people of unbelievers. The strength of the two groups may vary, but they have existed, side by side, from the beginning, combating but at the same time stimulating and staving up each other.

Was Joseph, the head of the family into which Jesus was born, one of those who serve God by their obedience or of those who by their defiance challenge God to make God known? Did he love and fear God and strive to carry out all the *mitzvot*, or commandments of the Law, or did he go to the synagogue only on Yom Kippur, the Day of Atonement, and, in spite of the rabbi's exhortations, stay away until the following year?

We have every reason to believe that Joseph and Mary were practicing Jews. Their annual trip to Jerusalem and their contribution to the treasury of the Temple show that they made a particular effort to follow the precepts of their religion. The Gospel according to Luke tells us that after Jesus was born Mary observed the rite of purification, according to the law of Moses. She and Joseph took the child to Jerusalem to consecrate him to the Lord, and following the orders of Leviticus they made an offering of two turtledoves. We have no reason to doubt their piety.

We may imagine, then, that Joseph carried out the prescriptions of the Law not only in the synagogue but in his own house as well. On the doorpost of his modest dwelling there was a *mezuzah*, a roll of parchment inside a metal tube, on it the fundamental Jewish prayer, the Shema: "*Shema, Israel, Adonai elohenu, Adonai ehad*" (Hear, O Israel; the Lord our God, the Lord is one). This meant that the house was consecrated, in obedience to the injunction found in Deuteronomy:

> . . . *These words, which I command you this day, shall be in your heart:*
>
> *And you shall teach them diligently to your children, and shall talk of them when you sit in your house, and when you walk by the way, and when you lie down, and when you rise up.*
>
> *And you shall bind them for a sign upon your hand, and they shall be as frontlets between your eyes.*
>
> *And you shall write them upon the posts of your houses and on your gates.*

Hence the mezuzah on the doorpost, the phylacteries worn on the forehead and the back of the left hand and the daily recital of the above verses. Joseph practiced other domestic rites as well. For one thing, he ate kosher food. In Acts 10:14, Saint Peter tells us: "I have never eaten anything that is profane or unclean." Since Peter must often have taken meals at Jesus' side, we may deduce that Jesus too observed the dietary laws. Some of these may be attributed to sanitary considerations, such as the prohibition of pork, natural in a hot country. But others have a religious origin. The ban against eating the sciatic nerve of any slaughtered animal comes from the fact that Jacob was wounded in this part when he wrestled with the angel. As for the taboo on blood, this is straight from Leviticus 17:14:

> For the life of every creature—its blood is its life; therefore I have said to the people of Israel: You shall not eat the blood of any creature, for the life of every creature is its blood; whoever eats it shall be cut off.

Wine, too, is the object of ritual prescriptions. Kosher wine is no different from any other, but every hand that has touched it, from that of the grape picker to that of the bottler, is a Jewish hand. Under these conditions wine is not only drunk, informally, at every meal, but it serves also for the Kiddush, or blessing, with which the head of the family pays homage at the beginning of every Sabbath to the Eternal:

> Blessed are you, O Lord our God, King of the Universe, who created the fruit of the vine.

The child Jesus also wore the clothing prescribed by the Law. After he was three years old his coat bore the *sisit*, or fringe, ordained in Deuteronomy 22:12: "You shall make tassels on the four corners of the cloak with which you cover yourself."

Food and clothing, these two fundamentals of a child's early years, were impregnated, in the young Jesus' eyes, with a religious meaning that transcended and transfigured their mere everyday function. Another thing that sanctified the life of the humble house was an abundance of benedictions.

Every action, no matter how commonplace, called forth Joseph's blessing. We must remember that the Jewish world is completely sacred; even its most earthy aspects are joined to the divine, and if Jews are to participate in this mixed natural and supernatural order they must, in every passing circumstance, praise the Lord.

"Whosoever enjoys some pleasure of the senses without offering a benediction," says the Talmud, "commits a sacrilegious theft against God."

The *berakhah*, or benediction, is the ever reforged tie that binds us to God. "The earth is the Lord's and all that is in it," according to Psalm 24:1, but when consecrated by a benediction it becomes our privilege to enjoy it. Hence the ritual form of every blessing, which must invoke both the name of God and the attribute to God's kingship. Every blessing begins with the same words: "*Baruk atta Adonai, Elohenuh melek ha-olam . . .*" (Praised be thou, O Lord our God, Ruler of the Universe). Hence, also, the number and variety of benedictions. Every casual event, every voluntary action is an occasion to thank and glorify God. For the course of an ordinary day the sages of Israel have set up a hundred benedictions that every Jew ought to pronounce between the rising and the setting of the sun. "Like the hundred sockets which held up the sanctuary in the wilderness, so the hundred daily *berakhot* hold up the sanctuary of our life."

So it is that as soon as they wake up, Jews bless God who, in the words of the psalm, "stretched out the earth above the waters"; they bless God while getting dressed; as they lace their shoes they praise God for having "supplied me with every want," and as they put on their belts they call upon the Eternal who "girds Israel with might." This benediction, like many others, has an allegorical meaning. In buckling a belt to hold up our lower garments we not only recall our double nature, but we hide our lower organs from the organs above so that we may easily drive all impure thoughts from our minds.

A benediction for every meal, a benediction for going to bed, a benediction for even the humblest bodily functions, which in this way are tied up with the order of the universe.

"Praise to the Lord our God, Ruler of the Universe who formed men and women in wisdom and created many orifices . . . who heals all flesh."

And, on a higher plane, a benediction upon God for having given us the Law, for having allowed us to participate in the Covenant:

"Praise to the Eternal Ruler of the Universe, who has not made me a heathen."

A blessing for liberty:

"Praise to the Lord God, Ruler of the Universe, who has not made me a slave."

A blessing for that orderliness of the world in which even animals participate:

"Praise to the Lord God, Ruler of the Universe, who has given the cock intelligence to distinguish between night and day."

If the sun is out, God is to be blessed for its beneficent rays; if there are thunder and lightning, God is to be thanked for safekeeping and if it rains, for the benefit to the crops.

And so benedictions followed the child Jesus all through the day, and within the confines of his family's house he was made aware of a whole universe dedicated to God. Every one of his thoughts and acts was colored by a consciousness of divinity. The intimacy with God he acquired with his first stammered words, his earliest awakening to the world, would never desert him. And when, for the first time, Joseph took him by the hand and led him to the house of prayer, the synagogue, he entered upon the discovery of still more ties with the divine.

Jesus' first entrance into the synagogue of Nazareth was the encounter of the founder of a new religion with the practices of one already old, which have remained practically the same up to the present day. A contemporary Christian, visiting a synagogue, would hear many of the prayers with which Jesus was familiar.

The synagogue is a house not only of prayer but of study, and sometimes is even referred to as a school. Often the Law is taught in a room adjoining that used for the divine service. But the synagogue is not a sanctuary. The Temple of Jerusalem, even after its destruction, is the only place entitled to this name. The synagogue by its half sacred, half profane character, symbolizes the paradox of Israel, a people chosen by God and yet living in the world in the same way as any other.

In its lack of ritual and clericalism the synagogue is a specifically Jewish institution. It is a body of believers gathered together to pray and learn, without benefit of clergy, since any one of its members can officiate on behalf of the rest. Rabbis are not professional priests, but people who love God and have studied God's Law; they watch over the service but do not conduct it alone. They may explain the Scriptures from the pulpit, but any member of the congregation, or even a visitor, is empowered to do the same thing. Nothing distinguishes rabbis from the rest of the faithful; the *tallith*, or prayer shawl, confers no rank upon them, but is merely the garment they put on as they do, for the sake of reverence, in addressing a public prayer to God. The service is simply an act of worship, performed by congregants meeting as friends or neighbors together. We know from the Gospels that Jesus often condemned the Jewish ritualism of his time. But he attacked practices of the Temple at Jerusalem, not of the local synagogue.

For it was in the synagogue that he was initiated into Jewish life and then, over a period of thirty years, felt the ripening of his predestined vocation. In the synagogue, likewise, after his ministry had begun, he delivered his personal interpretation of the Law and clashed with the Pharisees. It was to the Pharisees, however, that the synagogue owed its development, and the synagogue, during periods of persecution and dispersion, preserved the Jews' monotheistic heritage from destruction. Later, it served as a model for the first Christian communities and continued to exist, with unabated vitality, until our own day.

For the synagogue, or rather the synagogues, are separate from the Temple of Jerusalem; over the centuries they have alternately supplemented and replaced it. Jewish tradition takes the synagogue all the way back to Mount Sinai. As soon as Moses came down with the Ten Commandments there was a beginning of the teaching of the Law. The Shema enjoins the teaching of the Torah, and this can only mean that every Jewish community should have a meeting place and hence a synagogue.

The Temple held a different and unique place in the story of the Jewish people. It was served by a clerical hierarchy, composed not of rabbis but of priests. Here were offered up the sacrifices that the synagogues did no more than gather together or else replace by prayers; here was the seat of the supreme religious authority. The synagogues, on the other hand, were more like parochial associations, which held to the fundamental dogma but enjoyed considerable organizational autonomy. The majesty of the Temple and of its ceremonies was in sharp contrast to the rustic simplicity of the synagogues. Obviously there was no rivalry between them, but during the periods when the Temple did not exist the synagogues, less conspicuous and hence less vulnerable, served as repositories of the Jewish faith, and by their very nature they promoted individual prayer rather than elaborate ceremony.

It was between 587 and 539 B.C. during the Jews' Babylonian exile, that the synagogues first assumed importance, taking the place of the destroyed Temple and basing a religious life on prayer rather than on sacrifice. The synagogues developed, from then on, in periods of persecution and dispersion, the two fatally recurrent conditions of Israel's existence.

In the fourth century B.C., when the Jewish nation was once more gathered together and the Temple rebuilt, Esdras, Nehemiah and other sages of the time reorganized Jewish worship. They emphasized the study of the Torah and the role of prayer, as the synagogues had developed them. And so, in spite of the reconstruction of the Temple, the synagogues continued to flourish, and soon every village had one of its own. Even in Jerusalem itself there were variously estimated to be between 384 and 480 synagogues. Their function was so different from that of the Temple that there was one within the Temple itself, in the *Lishkath hagazith*, or Chamber of Hewn Stone, where the Sanhedrin assembled. Here the form of worship was composed entirely of the prayers that in the Temple were pronounced only between sacrifices. The reading of the Law took place not only in the sacred language of Hebrew, but also in the spoken tongue, Aramaic. In the shadow of the newly rebuilt sanctuary, which was doomed soon to fall again, the synagogue represented the permanence of the personal and intimate religious feeling of the Jewish people. The Pharisees, who were its sponsors, had little in common with the more ritualistic sect of the Sadducees, from whose numbers came most of the professional clergy.

So we may imagine Joseph, leading Jesus to the synagogue school, or *Bet ha-keneset*, as it is called in Hebrew. This was a bare, rectangular room, with no decorational motif other than the Star of David or the seven-branched candlestick (really a lamp), since representation of the divinity was forbidden. The only pieces of furniture were those used for worship. First, against one of the shorter sides of the rectangle, the Ark (Aron Hakodesh) containing the scroll of the Torah (Sepher Torah). This was several steps above the floor, and on the top step there was a reading desk, the *tebah*, at which the officiant took their place in order to say their prayers face to face with the word of God. In the center of the room there was a platform, known as the *bimah* or *almemor*, where the scroll of the Law was taken to be read aloud.

The faithful sat on benches, facing the Ark, which was orientated toward the Temple of Jerusalem. Before the Ark there was a perpetually burning lamp, emblem of the spiritual light that God sheds upon people. And inside, as we have said before, the Sepher Torah, the parchment scroll on which a scribe (*sopher*) had copied the text of the Pentateuch. Every time, in the course of their copying, that the scribes came to the name of God they interrupted their work to say: "I shall consecrate my writing to the holiness of God's name." Certain scribes were so scrupulous that they took a ritual bath in order to purify the hand with which they held the pen.

The Sepher Torah was rolled around two wooden sticks, each with disks at top and bottom, in whose grooves were inscribed the names of both the donor and the scribe. It was wrapped in a precious cloth bearing the image of the Lion of Judah or the Seal of Solomon and the words: "The Crown of the Torah," and protected by a silver plaque, the *tags*. At the most solemn moment of a Sabbath or Holy Day service, the officiant removed the Torah from the Ark and, followed by the notables of the congregation, carried it through the synagogue. The faithful crowded around, touching the precious cloth with a corner of their prayer shawls and then kissing the corner. During the procession tiny silver bells were hung from the upper disks of the sticks holding the scroll, reminiscent of the bells that decked the high priest's robes during a ceremony at the Temple. Another ritual object was the *yad*, a sculptured hand at the end of a rod, which served the reader of the *parashah*, or text for the day, as a pointer. The removal of the Torah from the Ark and its replacement therein were accompanied by chanting in which the whole congregation took part.

This was the simple but impressive ceremony by which every Jew was made familiar with the Law of God. And it was to a synagogue such as the one we have just described that Joseph introduced Jesus as a young child. In all likelihood he took him there at least three times a week: on the Sabbath (Friday evening and Saturday) and on the two other days—Monday and Thursday—when the Torah was read. And, of course, on the great traditional holidays, the anniversaries that are a compendium of Jewish theology. Passover, the first day of the religious year, commemorative of the Children of Israel's deliverance from Egypt; Rosh Hashanah, the Feast of Trumpets, anniversary of the Creation and civil New Year's Day; Yom Kippur, the dusk-to-dusk day of atonement, when, until he was thirteen years old, Jesus fasted only half as long as the adults; and also on the feasts of Shavuot (Weeks) or Pentecost, commemorative of the gift of the Law; and Succot (Tabernacles), Thanksgiving. Passover, Pentecost and Tabernacles were originally agrarian festivals, since Passover marked (in the Holy Land's hot climate) the beginning of the harvest, Pentecost its end and Tabernacles the gathering-in of the grapes for wine. They still have vestiges of their rustic character.

We can imagine Joseph, on his bench, putting on his prayer shawl for the reading of the Law, but otherwise simply dressed in his best clothes. His head was covered, in order to show his respect and fear of the Lord, but also as a mark of the special destiny God gave to Israel by "crowning it with glory." Beside him sat the child Jesus, also with covered head, attentive at some moments to what was going on but at others, like his contemporaries, wearied by the interminable length of prayers said in a language, Hebrew, which he did not yet know. On the Sabbath, when Joseph, with his prayer shawl over his head, was called to the Torah to read the *parashah* for the week, Jesus opened his eyes wide and sat proudly next to the seat left empty beside him. But at other times, with some mischievous boys of his own age, he slipped out from among the adults and went to play on the steps of the *tebah*. At his quieter moments he dreamed, perhaps, of the day of his religious coming-of-age, of his thirteenth birthday and bar mitzvah, when he would be empowered to publicly read the Sabbath service from beginning to end.

The village house of prayer had, then, an atmosphere almost as intimate as that of his own home, and even if he did not know the meaning of all the Hebrew words, their sound was familiar to him. The song of the birds and the smell of the fields, wafted through the wide-open doors, took the place of organ and incense respectively. Behind him, in the space set aside for the women, he could see Mary, his mother.

The regular weekly service began simply, when one of those present put on a prayer shawl and mounted the *tebah*. But on more ceremonial occasions there were preliminaries, beginning in the home. Before even setting out for the synagogue the head of the family pronounced this invocation:

"How goodly are thy tents, O Jacob, thy tabernacles, O Israel! Through thy great mercy, O God, I come to thy House . . . O Lord, I love the place of thy house and the abode in which thy glory dwells. And so I bow down, and adore thee, O God, my Maker. . . ."

Then came the "song of degrees" as he went on:

"My foot stands in an even place; in the congregations will I bless the Lord."

And finally the hymn of David:

"But we will bless the Lord from this time forth and for evermore. Praise the Lord."

The festal service began with the Barekhu, the solemn benediction, which is still one of its outstanding points today:

"Praise ye the Lord, to whom all praise is due.

"Praised be the Lord, to whom all praise is due for ever and ever."

It was a decisive moment in Jesus' religious career when he began to say *Amen*. For as the Talmud tells us: "The child wins a part of his future salvation when he learns to say *Amen*."

Jesus learned also to distinguish the prayers offered at various hours of the day. There are three separate offices, beginning with that of the twilight (which is when the world was created), known as Arvit or Maariv, and going on to Shahrit, or the office of the dawn, and finally to Minhah (literally, offering), the office of the afternoon. According to the Talmud, the morning office was instituted by Abraham, the afternoon one by Isaac, and that of the evening by Jacob.

Among these three patriarchs Abraham stands alone, by far the most glorious, or rather the one with the most untarnished glory. Possessing every blessing, he was neither envied nor hated but was venerated as a prince of God.

Isaac's place is less secure, for he was a solitary man, whose contemporaries were jealous of him, with the result that he was pushed back into himself and his own family. In Isaac was fulfilled God's prophecy to Abraham: "Your seed shall be a stranger in a land that is not yours," which was to be the fate of all Israel.

As for Jacob, his lot was the hardest of all. His life was painful and good fortune rarely came his way or lasted for long.

These three just men, these three *zaddikim,* in spite of their very different lives, all found their way to God through prayer, and this is why they inspire the three offices of the Jewish day. By the same token, each one of these offices has a different tone from the others and represents a particular episode in the drama of the Jewish vocation.

In Shahrit, the office of the dawn, commemorative of Abraham, Nature bursts forth in all the brilliance of youth from the shadows of night. With the rising sun people attain fulfillment of their being and of all the possibilities their freedom allows them. During the night, people, "the earthly masters of creation," are bound by the same chains as those of the universe, but every morning they throw these chains off anew. As the Kabbalah tells us: "Daytime is the reign of God's love, which gives man full possession of his freedom and resources, in order that, by perfecting himself, he may become an image of God." Daytime is the time of God's grace, and in their first prayer the Jews thank God for it.

> Blessed are you, O Lord our God, King of the Universe, who has sanctified us by your commandments.

In the evening, on the other hand, people are caught up in darkness, they are the passive victims of the cosmos. Helpless victims of the forces of Nature, they look not for God's grace but for God's mercy. What a contrast there is between the morning and evening prayers! The former is in a key of exultation:

> Blessed is the Lord who is to be blessed for ever and ever.
> Blessed are you, O Lord our God, King of the Universe, who forms light and creates darkness, who makes peace and creates all things:
> Who in mercy give light to the earth and to them that dwell upon it, and in your goodness renews the creation continually . . .
> O cause a new light to shine upon Zion, and may we all be worthy soon to enjoy its brightness. Blessed are you, O Lord, Creator of the luminaries.

> *With abounding love have you loved us, O Lord our God,*
> *with great and exceeding pity have you pitied us. O our Father,*
> *our King, for our fathers' sake, who trusted in you, and whom you*
> *taught the statutes of life, be also gracious to us and teach us . . .*
>
> *Enlighten our eyes in your Law, and let our hearts cleave to*
> *your commandments, and unite our hearts to love and fear your*
> *name, so that we be never put to shame.*
>
> *Because we have trusted in your holy, great and revered name,*
> *we shall rejoice and be glad in your salvation.*

Whereas the evening prayer expresses resignation and obedience:

> *Blessed are you, O Lord our God, King of the Universe, who*
> *with a word brings on the evening twilight, with wisdom opens the*
> *gates of the heavens, and with understanding changes times and*
> *varies the seasons, and arranges the stars in their watches in the*
> *sky, according to thy will. You create day and night; you roll away*
> *the light from before the darkness, and the darkness from before the*
> *light; you make the day to pass and the night to approach, and*
> *divide the day from the night, the Lord of Hosts is your name; a*
> *God living and enduring continually, may you reign over us for*
> *ever and ever. Blessed are you, O Lord, who brings on the evening*
> *twilight.*

Between these two offices, the awakening to day and the acceptance of night, the afternoon office of Minhah has a no less essential role to play. It takes place at the end of the working day, which may have been fraught with temptation and sin, and constitutes a balancing of accounts whose importance the Talmud particularly stresses. It is when God hears the prayers of the Minhah that God decides whether or not people deserve an answer to all the hopes, wishes and petitions that they have expressed during the daylight hours. At this time, before night has descended, people seek to make their peace with God. They offer up the actions of the day, upon whose worthiness depends the tranquility of the night's sleep that lies ahead.

Shahrit, Minhah, Maariv, these three groups of prayer, by which, every day, Jews obey God and fit themselves into the pattern of the universe, must have made Jesus feel that there is no such thing as a profane hour. Just as every spoken word calls up an aspect of God and every accomplished act lights a sacred spark from the matrix of inert Nature, so every minute of the day was sanctified. For Jesus, as for his fellow Jews, every recurrence of the cycle of prayer recalled the intimate bonds between God and creation, and all the symbolic acts attached to them.

When Moses approached God on Mount Sinai, he passed through three successive zones, of darkness, fog and cloud, symbolized by the three daily offices of Jewish worship and also by the three steps all Jews take when they approach the Shekhina, the divine Presence, the abode of the Most High, and the three backward steps when their prayers are over.

Here we have seen some of the complex feelings that Jesus must have entertained when he entered the synagogue at Joseph's side and waited to hear him pray. The synagogue was a very real, everyday place where he and the other children of his age were alternately attentive or disorderly, murmuring snatches of prayer in a language they did not understand or else scuffling in the time-honored manner of schoolchildren when they are unable to take in what is going on around them. But at the same time the synagogue was a place of transfiguration, where every word had an echo, every motion a reason and every hour some significance. A house for the sanctification of time, a house of study and prayer, where the atmosphere was charged with all the joys and sorrows of life.

Let us imagine the child Jesus emerging from the simplicity of his family life into the mystery of the community religion. At this time he must have experienced and accepted the destiny of Israel's mission.

CHAPTER FOUR

The Child Jesus before God

THE CHILD JESUS, AS the Gospel according to Luke tells us, "The child grew and became strong, filled with wisdom; and the favor of God was upon him." These words refer to the time when he was twelve years and approaching his religious initiation, the bar mitzvah, which marked a young Jew's complete admission to the community of Israel. Once this solemnity was accomplished Jesus would be considered an adult; he could count as one of the ten men required to be present at a service in the synagogue. The bar mitzvah is not a baptism, confirmation or blessing; there is no great mystery about it. When he became thirteen years old, having prepared himself for several months before by learning the appropriate prayers and passages of the Torah, Jesus went to the synagogue, wearing for the first time the *tallith*, or prayer shawl, and for the first time he conducted the Sabbath service. From this time on he was to take part in Israel's mission and, like every other Jew, to be a priest. For God had said to Moses: "you shall be for me a priestly kingdom and an holy nation" (Exodus 19:6). But his priesthood was to have a lay character, since the synagogue had no clergy.

Jesus was now empowered to "officiate," that is to mount the *tebah*, turn toward the Ark of the Covenant, pronounce benedictions, read the weekly *parashah*, or prescribed passage from the Pentateuch, sing alternate verses of the psalms with the congregation and carry on his youthful shoulders the scroll of the Law in solemn procession. For none of these tasks did he require any special consecration. God's covenant with the chosen people, from the time of Abraham, was an all-sufficient investiture. At the same time, Jesus' new position with regard to God in no way took him away from the company of other people. Israel had another priest, but the Jewish nation had not lost a lay citizen.

If we knew the exact date of Jesus' birth and hence that of his bar mitzvah, we could find the passage of the Pentateuch appointed for reading during the week when he mounted the *tebah* for the first time. This might furnish us further clues to his spiritual itinerary. But all we know is the nature of his long preparation for the great day. These fall into two categories of study, which in the Jewish mind are closely akin: the first connected with the history of the Jewish people and the second with prayer and the Torah.

The history of Israel is written in the Pentateuch, the first five books of the Bible, and in Judges, Kings and Chronicles, the three most important ones to follow. In the synagogue it is treated in two ways. First, every Saturday there is a reading of the weekly *sidra* or *parashah*. This is a didactic process, which evokes the high points of Israel's story: the Creation, the Flood, the calling of Abraham, the years in Egypt, the Exodus, the passage of the Red Sea, the revelation of Mount Sinai, the promulgation of the Law, the worship of the Golden Calf, the rebellion of Korah and, finally, the last words of Moses and his prophetic benediction. The weekly readings of this story begin with the first chapter of Genesis and end with the last chapter of Deuteronomy, passing through Exodus, Leviticus and Numbers on the way. From century to century the reading has proceeded at a different pace; in our day it takes a little over a year and includes fifty-four *parashiyyot*, but at the time of Jesus it seems that it was divided into 175 episodes and lasted three years. If this is so, then between the ages of five and twelve he would have twice heard the whole cycle, from the creation of Adam to the death of Moses. With every Sabbath the destiny of Israel must have been impressed more deeply upon his mind. Let us look for a moment at the last *parashah*, the farewell to Moses:

> *And there arose not a prophet since in Israel like unto Moses, whom the Lord knew face to face,*
>
> *In all the signs and the wonders, which the Lord sent him to do in the land of Egypt to Pharaoh, and to all his servants and to all his land.*
>
> *And in all that mighty hand, and in all the great terror which Moses showed in the sight of all Israel.*

Like many another Jew, but perhaps more so, Jesus must have regretted that the story should end here and then start over again. Why not go on? Why should the period after the death of the first prophet and periods still more recent be left out of the weekly commemoration? Was God's time divided into separate zones, with a wall between them? Why not look over the wall and add new chapters to the divine book? Like other Jews animated by the Messianic spirit, Jesus must have asked himself questions such as these.

Of course the synagogue has, in the course of history, tried to adorn and brighten the return to the beginning of the Pentateuch cycle. It has been made to follow after Yom Kippur, as if to signify that only after purification by fasting can the faithful make a fresh start. It has been glorified by the addition of a special ceremony, the Simhat Torah, during which a procession of children winds its way clamorously through the synagogue, brandishing the scroll of the Law, ever old and ever new. Perhaps Jesus himself took part in some such demonstration.

But whatever gaiety attended upon the return to the beginnings, Jesus may have continued to think longingly of the future. He may even have imagined a "176th parashah," never yet read or interpreted, which would give Jewish worship an outlet into the future. Perhaps as he followed the services held in the synagogue of Nazareth, Jesus dreamed of writing, of living, this "176th parashah" himself.

In any case, as we have just seen, Jews of Jesus' time made their first contact with the history of Israel through the didactic readings of the Pentateuch. The synagogue's second treatment of this history is less bookish, more familiar and specifically Jewish in character. It consists of reviving and reliving history by means of a series of religious holidays, each one of them reminiscent of a past event. Rosh Hashanah commemorates the Creation; Passover the exodus from Egypt; Pentecost (Shavuot) the gift of the Law; Tabernacles (Succot) includes two symbolic rites: first that of the *succah* (the "booth" or grass tent, in which the Children of Israel sojourned in the desert), where there is a blessing of the season's wine, and second, that of the *lulav*, a bundle of palm, myrtle and willow branches, held together with a citron, and shaken in the direction of the four points of the compass as a reminder of God's goodness to Israel. Among the minor feasts are Hanukkah, which celebrates the rebuilding of the temple after the victory of Judas Maccabeus, and Purim (Lots), in honor of Esther's triumph over the cruel Haman, one of the first men in history who tried to exterminate the Jews.

And so every religious holiday is an evocation of the past, an evocation of a down-to-earth kind, which it is hard to imagine outside Judaism, not so much a retelling of the story as a reliving of it. The commemorations of modern times glorify, as wholeheartedly as they can, a dead hero or a great deed of the past. But the gap of time leaves the participants with a feeling of detachment. No matter how elaborate are the parades, how eloquent the speeches, the hero is only a dead man and the event of a hundred years ago cannot be brought to life. This fits in with the Greek and Roman conception of time, in which past, present and future occupy fenced-off areas and the path between them is one-way and can never be retraced.

For the Jew of biblical days, to celebrate a past event meant to relive it; to honor dead heros meant to resurrect them. A Jewish commemoration is essentially a reenactment. Jews who take part in it, although they know that the past is dead and buried, feel themselves close to and almost in the skin of their great predecessor. He is Adam, driven from the Garden of Eden, Noah building the Ark, Moses on Mount Sinai, Abraham receiving God's order to leave everything and go accomplish his mission.

To compare a deep religious experience with a contemporary criminological procedure, we may say that a Jewish commemorative ceremony is like the police's attempt to obtain a murderer's confession by making the murderer reenact the crime. In the course of the religious rite the participants are plunged into the past. This is obvious, in a naive but convincing manner, in the role they play in the celebration.

Let us take, for instance, Purim. The greater part of the service, which glorifies the victory of the Jew, Mordecai, over the persecutor, Haman, consists of a reading of the Megillah, or scroll, containing the Book of Esther. During this reading the listeners are not in the least passive; they are not like schoolchildren, who know the end of an oft-told tale and pay no attention to it. To them every episode of the drama is very much alive. They are afraid that things may go badly, that Mordecai may be overcome or Esther repudiated. With every fiber of their being they strive to contribute to the defeat of Haman, who they know is the forerunner of other persecutors. As we have seen earlier, at every mention of his name the children stamp their feet, as if he were present among them and they were trying to scare him away. May we not imagine that in the first days of Christianity, before Synagogue and Church were separated, Jewish children, loyal to Jesus, stamped their feet in the same way at the name of Judas?

There is another and still more significant example. The Hebrew word *Pesach* (Passover) means a passage from the natural to the supernatural order. Humans are creatures of this passing-over; their role is that of a link between the Creator and creation. In the life of Jesus the Passover has a recurring importance. It was on the occasion of the Passover that Jesus went, at the age of twelve, to Jerusalem and, according to Luke, met the doctors. Once his bar mitzvah was accomplished, we may imagine that he made the same journey every year. And after the hidden years were over and he had been baptized by Saint John, the Gospels record four Passover celebrations. Is it not highly significant that the Last Supper, the prelude to the Passion, was a repetition of the Seder, the ritual meal that Jewish families ate together on the eve of the Passover?

For Jesus, as for the other Jews of his time, the Passover was the crowning point of the religious year, the time when history was the most vividly alive in their conscience. At this moment the *berith*, the covenant, was closest to them; as they sat at the supper table they were more than ever aware that it had never been abolished. And what is the exact nature of the Passover celebration? It is celebrated in two different ways: publicly, in the synagogue, and privately, in the home.

The Passover celebration in the synagogue is one of the most striking pieces of Jewish liturgy in its richness and diversity. There are prayers and benedictions that, as in any religious service, mark the sacred aspect of the rite; these are like the spires of a cathedral, stretching up to heaven. But in the early centuries of a faith, when sanctuaries are built and liturgies come into being, this heavenward aspiration does not prevent, indeed it positively favors the thrust of roots into the ground. A Gothic cathedral, it has been said, is a Bible in stone, in whose stained glass and sculpture even the illiterate can find everything they need to know, not only to worship God but also to live in the world. For alongside the images of God and God's saints there are familiar, even sensual scenes. When the cathedrals were built, religion was much less conventional than it is now.

Jewish liturgy, particularly that of the Passover, is in this domain a forerunner of the Gothic cathedral. The most solemn prayers are harmoniously mingled with expressions of love and adoration, which are not in the least disincarnate and ethereal but, on the contrary, earthy, fleshly and closely tied to human nature and history. The office is a melody, with the same themes recurring, not in a logical sequence but according to an inwardly meaningful plan. First, the theme of the exodus from Egypt, developed in a series of short litanies. These have doubtless been added to over the centuries, but since they are inspired by the *midrash*, which was already in formation at Jesus' time, we may say that he would have understood their feeling.

On Passover the affliction of the faithful was decreed for a
span of four hundred years, on the days of the Passover . . .
On Passover He slayed Ham's firstborn, but upon His own
first-born he had compassion, on the days of the Passover.

> *The Passover was ordained for judgment of evildoers, and that*
> *thereon saviors should go up to Zion, as on the days of the*
> *Passover.*
>
> *On Passover He wove destruction about the foe, and redeemed*
> *His cherished sons from bondage, on the days of the Passover . . .*

Here we have a brief summary of the commemorated events, which return again and again in prayers and benedictions. Later on in the service there is a more detailed treatment, taken from Nehemiah:

> *You saw the affliction of our fathers in Egypt, and heard their*
> *cry by the Red Sea.*
>
> *And showed signs and wonders upon Pharaoh, and on all his*
> *servants, and on all the people of his land: for you knew that they*
> *deal proudly against them. So did you get a name as it is this day.*
>
> *And you divided the sea before them, so that they went*
> *through the midst of the sea on the dry land; and you threw*
> *their persecutors into the depths, as a stone into the mighty*
> *water.*

And the *parashah* for Passover is, of course, taken from the chapters of Exodus relating the escape from Egypt and the passage of the Red Sea. This historical theme is intertwined with the great liturgical prayers—the Shema, the Barekhu, the Shemoneh-Esreh, the Alenu—forming a part, but not all, of their human accompaniment. Because for the people of Israel, crowding the synagogues, as for the Christians crowding their cathedrals, every form of worship had its familiar side. In this Jewish solemnity, which has history for a connecting thread, spiritual exaltation and physical incarnation are found side by side. In a portion of the Passover office inspired by The Song of Solomon, God is the lover to whom Israel, the beloved, addresses a song of love.

I am black but comely . . .
My beloved is mine and I am his . . .
My beloved is like the hart and the young roe; my God of
mercy goes before me . . .
My flesh and my heart pine for him . . .
My beloved is white and ruddy, an ensign among his hosts . . .
My beloved is altogether lovely; his judgments are true, sweet
and pleasant . . .

This intimacy with God, expressing itself in the language of human love, extends to the whole of the body. Jews, feeling themselves in the physical presence of God, fall into the posture of the loved one before the lover.

We now offer for Your devotion every individual limb in our
body, with the spirit and breath which You have blown in our nos-
trils, with the tongue in our mouth. With all these we thank,
laud, praise, glorify, revere, hallow and assign sovereignty to Your
Name, O our King. For every mouth shall give thanks to you,
and every tongue shall swear loyalty to you; every knee shall bow
to You and every body shall prostrate itself before You.

And so, as they celebrate the Passover, Jews are never disembodied or set apart from the world around them. The poetry of nature is added to that of love, and the universe vibrates in tune with the psalm:

When Israel went out of Egypt . . .
The sea saw it and fled; Jordan was driven back.
The mountains skipped like rams, and the little hills like lambs.

Unlikely, these words, if we take them literally. But in such figures of speech we have the real world, the land with which Jesus and the Jews of his time were so familiar that they could not help

both humanizing and deifying its everyday aspects. Even its secre-
tions spoke of God. For instance, the dew of the fields, symbolic of
God's covenant with humankind, inspires the following:

> *Dew, precious dew, unto Your land forlorn!*
> *Pour out our blessing in Your exultation,*
> *To strengthen us with ample wine and corn*
> *And give Your Chosen City safe foundation . . .*
> *For You are the Lord our God who causes the wind to blow*
> *and the dew to descend:*
> *For a blessing and not for a curse,*
> *For life and not for death,*
> *For plenty and not for famine.*

The synagogue's Passover liturgy is, then, firmly rooted in the
real world, in bodily and earthly aspirations as well as in the re-
creation of the past.

But there is another and more significant aspect of the Passover
celebration. The evening meal, the Seder, which Jesus must have
attended as a boy and young man before he made it the basis of his
Last Supper, has a capital part to play. Here, according to nineteenth-
century German poet Heinrich Heine, is the spirit in which it
should be prepared:

> *As soon as night falls, the mistress of the house lights the*
> *lamps, spreads the tablecloth, puts three pieces of the flat unleavened*
> *bread in its midst, covers them with a napkin, and on the pile*
> *places six little dishes containing symbolical food: an egg, lettuce,*
> *horseradish, the bone of a lamb, and a brown mixture of raisins,*
> *cinnamon, and nuts. At this table, the head of the house then sits*
> *down with all relations and friends, and reads to them from a very*
> *curious book called the Haggadah, the contents of which are a*
> *strange mixture of ancestral legends, miraculous tales of Egypt, odd*

narratives, disputations, prayers, and festive songs. A huge supper
is brought in halfway through this celebration; and even during the
reading, at certain times one tastes of the symbolic dishes, eats
pieces of unleavened bread, and drinks four cups of red wine.
This nocturnal festival is melancholically gay in character, gravely
playful, and mysterious as a fairy tale. And the traditional
singsong in which the Haggadah is read by the head of the house,
and now and then repeated by the listeners in chorus, sounds at
the same time so awesomely intense, maternally gentle, and
suddenly awakening, that even those Jews who have long forsaken
the faith of their fathers and pursued foreign joys and honors are
moved to the depths of their hearts when the old, familiar sounds
of the Passover happen to strike their ears.

Such is a poet's view of the outward trappings of the Seder.
Romantic as Heine's picture may seem, it is a faithful reproduc-
tion. The Seder's purpose is to call vividly to mind the flight from
Egypt, the end of Israel's bondage. In this context every detail is
significant. The unleavened bread, which becomes the sacred wafer
or host of the Christian rite, is reminiscent of the fugitives' fare:

Lo! This is the bread of affliction which our fathers ate in the
land of Egypt. Let all who are hungry come and eat. Let all who
are in want come and celebrate the Passover with us. This year we
celebrate it here, but next year we hope to celebrate it in the land of
Israel. This year we are bondsmen, but next year we hope to be free.

The bitter herbs, the horseradish, the parsley dipped in vinegar
or salt water, represent the bitterness of exile. The youngest member of the family asks:

Why is this night of Pesach so different from all other nights
of the year? On all other nights, we eat either leavened bread or
unleavened bread; why on this night, do we eat only matzoh,

*which is unleavened bread? On all other nights we eat vegetables
and herbs of all kinds; why on this night, do we eat bitter herbs
especially? On all other nights, we never think of dipping herbs in* ·
*water or in anything else; why on this night do we dip the parsley
in salt water and the bitter herbs in Haroset? On all other nights,
everyone sits up straight at the table; why on this night do we all
recline at the table?*

To these naive questions, which Jesus must have asked as a
child and answered as a young man, the head of the household
replies:

*We were Pharaoh's bondsmen in Egypt, and the Lord our
God delivered us with a mighty hand . . .*

The Lord our God delivered us. But this is not simply an event
of the past. For the liturgy defines the contemporary meaning of
the liberation:

*It is the duty of all Jews in every generation to regard them-
selves as though they personally had come out of Egypt. Not our
ancestors alone has the Holy One (praised be His name)
redeemed. "And He brought us out from thence, that He might
bring us in, to give us the land which He swore unto our fathers."*

Here, in its essential vigor, is the resurrection of history that
characterizes the Jewish religion. On this particular evening the
regular meal takes on an unusual significance and evokes the destiny
of Israel. The relationship between father and children is impregnated with tradition, and the wind of the spirit blows through the
odor of food and the clamor of conversation. This table is like any
other table, and yet it is one of a kind, symbolic of the ingenuous
and genuine fashion in which God has participated in Israel's history.
Here we have the tragicomic character of the race, its concrete
religiosity and its subtleties.

Among the more picturesque legends of the Haggadah is that of the kid, *Had Gadia*, symbolic of Israel, persecuted by infidels but eventually able, thanks to God's grace, to escape from them.

In the typically Hebraic form of the litany, the Haggadah contains a canticle of praise, built up from verse to verse. This is the thanksgiving whose refrain is "Dayyenu" (That would have sufficed us), signifying that God's kindness surpasses our expectation:

How many degrees of magnificence mighty conferred upon us!
If He had divided the sea for us and had not made us pass through it on dry land, Dayyenu.
If He had made us pass through its midst on dry land and had not sunk our oppressors into the sea, Dayyenu.
If He had sunk our oppressors into the sea and had not supplied our wants in the wilderness, Dayyenu.
If He had supplied our wants in the wilderness and had not fed us with manna, Dayyenu.
If He had fed us with manna and had not given us the Sabbath, Dayyenu.
If He had given us the Sabbath and had not brought us to Mount Sinai, Dayyenu.
If He had brought us to Mount Sinai and had not given us His law, Dayyenu.
If He had given us His law and had not led us into the land of Israel, Dayyenu.
If He had led us into the land of Israel and had not built the Temple, Dayyenu.

The family is gathered together, then, for the Passover meal, just as Jesus' disciples were gathered on the eve of the Passion. The prayers said on this occasion are born of casual, intimate conversation, and the food is an offering. Celebrants tell their own story, and all together they retell the story of Israel. It is difficult to say which part of the meal is sacred and which is profane. There is no mystery except that of human destiny; no liturgical element in the order of courses or of conversation. At this paschal meal God is the guest of the Jewish family, an unobtrusive guest who in this simple and intimate fashion is imprinted upon human history, a living God who takes part in the most commonplace and necessary of natural processes.

As always, in Israel, the present is filled with anticipation of the future. The door is left open, and there is an empty seat at the table, and a plate that will not need to be washed when the meal is over. This is the place prepared for Elijah, the prophet of the Messiah, and there is disappointment when he fails to occupy it, in spite of the fact that no one really thought that he would come. The coming of the Messiah is the most typical of Jewish myths, whose tangible reality is less important than its inner meaning. Everyone knows that Elijah will not show up before the end of the meal, but his appearance does not matter. What matters is that everything should proceed as if one day, perhaps this day or the next, he will come. The important thing in the reliving of Israel's history is not the succession of facts, but their significance. Let us leave to pagans and positivists the idolatrous conception of the miracle as a contradiction of natural law to which the Eternal must have recourse in order to demonstrate God's power. History is a never-ending miracle; we know that it will remain unfinished and yet we continue to hope that it will come to fruition. Life is a miracle, too, in spite of the commonplace means by which it is perpetuated. The Messiah is present at every moment, in every gesture by which life is made into history. Life is fleeting and history is incomplete, but the Messiah's place is always ready beside us, even if the Messiah never comes to occupy it.

Did Jesus save a place for Elijah at the Last Supper?

Or, after his disciples had gathered together, did he shut the door?

When Jesus was preparing for his bar mitzvah he also learned to pray.

Jewish prayer is not a petition addressed to God; it is support for the action of their Creator. Every prayer based on purely personal motives is habitually repressed. "Some men never receive an answer to their prayers," says the Sepher Hasidim, "because they are insensitive to the needs and misfortunes of others."

Because of human proneness to materialism and idolatry, Jewish prayer, like any other, may have a utilitarian and self-seeking aim. Even in the Psalms there are passages where the righteous are promised a reward. But this is not what prayer should be. Prayer concerns not the creature but the Creator. It reinforces God's power without offering any guarantee that it will be used to satisfy the desires of people.

When Israel is happy, it attributes its happiness to God and extols God's glory. When Israel experiences adversity, it does not think of its own honor but that of God. Israel's shame and triumph are also God's. Like David, Israel says: "Not to us, O Lord, not to us, but to your name give glory."

This is a forerunner of Jesus' ejaculation: "Thy will be done"; at the same time it underlines the effacement of men and women before God, which paradoxically causes them to share God's power.

In Jesus' time, and particularly at remote Nazareth, Jewish prayer was pure and severe. Among the prayers in use in the synagogue today it is possible to identify those which were in use two thousand years ago. Christians attending a Jewish service can be sure that some of the prayers they hear were said by Jesus in the course of those hidden years in which he studied the way to accomplish Israel's mission and his own.

As to the exact composition of the service in the synagogue during the period of the second Temple, when Jesus was alive, opinions may differ. There is no precise document to guide us. A prayer current today, the Lechah dodi greets the Sabbath in these amorous terms:

> Beloved, come, the bride to meet,
> The Princess Sabbath let us greet . . .

This prayer dates no further back than the sixteenth century. The age of others, such as the Alenu and the Kaddish, is debatable, but there are grounds for believing that they existed at Jesus' time. The Alenu is a prayer concerning Israel's universal mission, and at every divine service the faithful recite it:

> It is incumbent upon us to give praise to the Lord of the Universe, to glorify Him who formed creation, for He has not made us to be like the nations of the lands nor the families of the earth. He has not set our portion with theirs nor our lot with their multitude . . . Therefore do we wait for you, O Lord our God, soon to behold your mighty glory, when you will remove the abominations from the earth, and idols shall be exterminated . . .

According to rabbinical tradition, which is intuitive rather than factual, Joshua pronounced this prayer when he led the Children of Israel into the Promised Land. Some historians date it back to the period of the Second Temple, when Jesus was alive, but others attribute it to Abba Arika, a Babylonian rabbi of the third century.

As to the Kaddish, we have no proof of its date, but there is a strong likelihood that it goes back to the time of Jesus. As circumstantial evidence, we may mention the fact that it seems to have inspired the Lord's Prayer. This is a matter we shall take up in greater detail later on.

Three other prayers—the Shema, the Shemoneh-Esreh and the Barekhu—date back, without any doubt, to Jesus' time. We can be sure that, in the synagogue of Nazareth, Jesus recited them. The service began with the Ten Commandments, which were, however, eliminated before the end of the first century. Then came the Shema, the cornerstone of Jewish monotheism, which, apart from its place in the synagogue, every Jew must say morning and evening. The Shema, as we know, is composed of three passages from the Torah or Pentateuch and of three benedictions, two before and one after. The first passage is from the words spoken by Moses, in the book of Deuteronomy (6:4–9), after he had come down from Sinai with the Ten Commandments:

> *Hear, O Israel; The Lord our God, the Lord alone:*
> *You shall love the Lord your God with all your heart, and*
> *with all your soul, and with all your might.*
>
> *Keep these words that I am commanding you today in your*
> *heart.*
>
> *Recite them to your children and talk about them when you*
> *are at home, and when you are away, when you lie down, and*
> *when you rise up.*
>
> *Bind them as a sign on your hand, fix them as an emblem on*
> *your forehead, and write them on the doorposts of your house, and*
> *on your gates.*

To the young Jesus this beginning of the Shema was a historical pronouncement from the crucial point of his people's story; to say it was almost like singing a national anthem. This was no set of abstract precepts; it was the voice of Moses, perpetuated in the liturgy.

The second section of the prayer (Deuteronomy 11:13–15) is in Moses' words also. God has told Moses that if the Children of Israel obey the Law, "he will give grass in your fields for your livestock, and you will eat your fill." If, on the other hand, they "be seduced into turning away, serving other gods and worshiping them," if they commit Israel's besetting sin of idolatry, ". . . the anger of the Lord will be kindled against you and he will shut up the heavens, so that there will be no rain and the land will yield no fruit; then you will perish quickly off the good land that the Lord is giving you."

There is no question here of individual reward or punishment. Both the promise and the threat are addressed to the whole people, and at this historical moment we cannot dismiss them as products of superstition. It was an overwhelming fact that Israel's fate depended on its loyalty to the Covenant. People's individual destiny was linked with that of the nation, and the only thing they could do to better their own lot was to advance the mission of Israel. This is what the end of the second part of the Shema tells them:

> *Therefore shall you lay up these words in your heart and in your soul . . .*
>
> *That your days may be multiplied, and the days of your children, in the land which the Lord swore unto your fathers to give them, as the days of the heaven above the earth.*

After this confirmation of the bond between every son of Israel and the whole people, the third part of the Shema (Numbers 15:37–41) conveys some very precise instructions:

> *The Lord said to Moses:*
>
> *Speak to the Israelites, and tell them to make fringes on the corners of their garments throughout their generations and to put a blue cord on the fringe at each corner.*
>
> *You have the fringe so that, when you see it, you will remember all the commandments of the Lord and do them, and not follow the lust of your own heart and your own eyes.*
>
> *So you shall remember and do all my commandments, and you shall be holy to your God.*

I am the Lord your God, who brought you out of the land of Egypt, to be your God: I am the Lord your God.

As they pronounce the first verse of the Shema the officiants, who are turned toward the tabernacle, cover their eyes, to show that the sight of God is more than a person can bear. The congregation remains seated, because God's commands are not ecstatic or transcendent; they are made to the measure of the congregants, to be written into their doorposts and the hem of their garments.

The benedictions before and after the Shema take us into the realm of the *berakhot*, the expression of human support of the work of the Creator. In the first of the *berakhot* the officiant blesses God for giving light:

Blessed are you, O Lord our God, King of the Universe, who forms light and creates darkness, who makes peace and creates all things; who in mercy gives light to the world and to them that dwell therein; who in your goodness renews the work of creation every day continually, and who has arranged the lights in heaven, rejoicing the world which you have created: Blessed are you, O Lord, Creator of the luminaries.

In the second he thanks God for the gift of the Torah:

With abounding love have you loved us, O Lord our God, with great and exceeding pity have you pitied us, our Father, our King. O our Father, merciful Father, ever compassionate, have mercy upon us; O put it into our hearts to understand and to discern, to mark, learn and teach, to heed, to do and to fulfill in love all the words of instruction in your Law . . . It is us whom you have chosen out of all people and tongues; in love have you brought us near to your great Name, our King, that we may praise you and proclaim your unity: Blessed are you, who have chosen your people Israel in love.

These two blessings go before the Shema. The one that comes after it is in thanksgiving for the Covenant between God and Israel:

> *True, steadfast, firm, enduring, right, and faithful; beloved and precious, desirable and pleasant, revered and mighty, well-ordered and acceptable, good and beautiful is this word which you have spoken to us from of old and for evermore. You have been the support of our fathers, their Shield and Salvation, their Deliverer and Redeemer from of old. You are the first and you are the last, and beside you we have no King, Redeemer, or Savior. Blessed are you, O Lord, who redeems Israel.*

There are other benedictions besides those before and after the Shema, quite separate from it. The Shemoneh-Esreh, or Amidah, and the Barekhu mark the culminating point of the human impulse toward God. The Amidah is a silent prayer, now known also as the Shemoneh-Esreh (the Eighteen Blessings). In Jesus' time it was composed of only the first and last three of this number. The other twelve have been added throughout the years and do not have the same purity of intention as the original six, which constitute a participation in God's work. The first exalts the "God of our fathers, God of Abraham, God of Isaac and God of Jacob, the Creator of all, King, Helper, Savior and Shield." The second pays homage to God, as "sustaining the living and resurrecting the dead."

The third is in worship of God's holiness: "Blessed are You, O Lord, the Holy God."

The three final benedictions are also contributions to God's work, which do not ask anything from God. The sixteenth blesses God for the privilege of worshiping him "in fear." The seventeenth blesses God for accepting thanksgiving. The last, perhaps the most typical and most important, is concerned with peace: "Bestow peace . . . upon all Israel, your people . . . Bless us by the light of your countenance . . . Blessed are you, O Lord, who blesses your people Israel with peace."

A Talmudic scholar described this last benediction's relation to the world as that of leaven to dough, as the "motive force of human progress." The ancient Greeks seemed to look on war as the great leaven. But to the Jews, life is a perpetual struggle for peace. The very word *shalom* signifies both peace and well-being.

It is natural enough that the twelve intermediary benedictions, which we may presume to be later interpolations, should not have the same disinterested character. They presume to ask God's help for men and women—that God reveal true wisdom, ransom and forgive, exercise mental and physical healing, increase the harvest, gather in the exiles, and listen to prayers. At the time of the second Temple, the time of Jesus, in the village of Nazareth, where the Jewish faith was pure and simple, the worship of God did not ask for any blessing in return, except for the satisfaction a person might hope to feel from aiding and abetting God's work.

The Amidah, as we have indicated above, is said silently and in a standing position, to indicate that it is aimed unerringly at God and cannot fall back to the ground.

The Barekhu, the last prayer we can be sure that Jesus knew, is the most solemn and all-embracing, as well as the shortest, of all benedictions, consisting of two sentences, one spoken by the officiant:

"Praise you the Lord, to whom all praise is due."

To which the congregation responds:

"Praised be the Lord, to whom all praise is due for ever and ever."

In pronouncing these words Jesus, like any other Jew, bowed in the direction of the tabernacle, thereby backing up the prayer with the motion of his body. Every word, every gesture underlined total submission to God.

> *"Not to us, O Lord, not to us, but to your name give glory,*
> *for your mercy, and for your truth's sake."*

Such were the purity and disinterestedness of Jewish prayer at the time when Jesus was initiated into the religion of Israel. It was an uplifting of the spirit toward God, without distraction or calculation, a moment of harmony between people's condition on earth and what they glimpse of heaven. It might be almost too rarefied, were it not that the most glorious moments of Israel's history have a human context that makes them concrete and accessible. There is no screen, no intermediary between God and people. A *midrash* dating from Jesus' time, which recounts Moses' ascent of Mount Sinai, illustrates the intimacy between them.

> *When Moses started to climb the mountain where he was to receive the Law, some angels stopped him. "What are you doing here, miserable creature?" they asked. "Who gave you permission to enter the domain of purity?" To which Moses answered, quite simply: "I am a son of Abraham, and I have come on behalf of Israel to receive God's law." But the angels were not satisfied, and they breathed their burning breath upon him. "Master of the world," Moses implored. "I am afraid that they will burn me." And God answered reassuringly: "Seize the throne of my glory and you will find words to defend yourself." Having obtained God's support the prophet spoke to the angels in simple, human, common-sense terms, which quite disconcerted them. "Do you want to prevent me from receiving the Law?" he asked. "What business is it of yours? It's a Law made for human beings. And are you human? It is written in the Torah: 'Honor your father and your mother.' Have you father and mother? And it is further written: 'You shall not covet.' Have you ever coveted? The Torah*

*prescribes resting on the Sabbath day. Have you ever worked on
that day or any other? The Torah forbids adultery. And are there
any women among you? I say that the Law is not your affair."*

*Nonplussed by his human reasoning, the angels turned to
God. But he, in his turn, told his encumbering servitors some
hard truths. "Ever since you came into being," he said, "you've
prevented me from doing what I wanted . . . . When I wanted to
create the first man, you asked: 'What is he doing, that fellow?'
and gave me no peace until I had destroyed several of you . . .
Now you're beginning all over; you want to prevent me from giving Israel the Torah. Fools! Unless Israel receives the Torah there
will be no place in the universe for you, or even for me!"*

When Jesus heard this story, what a feeling of intimacy with
God it must have given him! The twelve years he spent at Nazareth
fell in an unusually pure and harmonious period of Jewish religious
history, when everything combined to give the feeling of that
peace that is epitomized in the word *shalom*. The landscape, the
social structure, the language, the liturgy all played their part. Jesus'
early years came at a time when the Jewish religion still had the
ingenuousness of its origins, as well as the lucid assurance of maturity. No doubt or anxiety, on the one hand; no weakness or
compromise or superstition on the other, but an atmosphere of
healthy balance; a strong faith and a tranquil mystery.

God's covenant with the chosen people, this unambiguous
contract so deeply rooted in history, to which each successive generation can write a codicil, gives every person a place to fill.
Another *midrash* text, a commentary on the Book of Job, sets forth
some wisdom capable of curing any human anxiety:

*Do not seek that which is beyond you. Do not seek to explore
that which is far away. That which is more marvelous than yourself you can never hope to know. Do not try to discover that which*

is hidden. Work to understand the heritage which God has given you. Nothing obscure or unrevealed need occupy your mind.

This commentary further develops the idea: "The secret things belong to the Lord our God" (Deuteronomy 29:29). The religion in which Jesus was instructed when he prepared for his bar mitzvah was a point of balance between mystery and reality. It is a wonderful thing to be on familiar terms with the ineffable, to be intimate with God.

PART TWO
Jerusalem

CHAPTER FIVE

The Arrival at Jerusalem

JESUS WENT, AT TWELVE years of age, with Mary and Joseph to Jerusalem. As he approached the city, conflicting feelings must have occupied his mind. On the one hand, joy at the possibility of becoming acquainted with the political and spiritual center of his country, on the other, sorrow that it should be in foreign hands.

Jerusalem was originally built at the border between two tribes, those of Benjamin and Judah, on a piece of stony ground, surrounded by hills. In the course of its growth like any other city, it absorbed a large number of villages around it. The Jerusalem of Jesus' time, under Roman occupation, consisted of three different sections, formerly independent one of the other. First the ancient town of Jebus, which King David won from the Jebusites. This was situated on a hill south of the future location of the Temple, but had originally no sanctuary of any kind. Second, the new city that David, the conqueror, built on Mount Zion, to the north. This was to be the seat of the Royal Palace and the Temple, the latter on the slopes of a foothill of Mount Zion, known as Moriah. Between the two hills, Jebus and Zion, was the valley of Millo, which David, and Solomon after him, had filled in so as to join the two settlements together. Third, a gradually developed new section along the ravine formed by the Brook Kidron.

Jerusalem lived and grew, like many another city, first under the impulsion of an energetic king, then as if by the spontaneous proliferation of its individual houses, until its stones and mud-daubed walls and pavements spread over all the space formerly occupied only by the springs of Gihon and Siloam. By Jesus' time the city had attained its maximum size; it had a circumference of about three miles. This was the length of the wall which the Roman emperor, Titus, threw up around it.

Within this enclosure, numbering a quarter of a million inhabitants, there were all sorts of historical sites. Most conspicuous, alas, the military installations that allowed the Roman conquerors to maintain order. On Mount Zion the fortress of Antiochus and the Tower of Antonia, at the northeast corner of the Temple, with a view over its every entrance and exit. But the Romans were concerned not only with security, but with convenience. Pilate's palace was almost next door to the northern facade of the Temple; Agrippa's palace rose on the east slope of Mount Zion, overhung by Golgotha; the palace of Herod, the collaborationist king, was not far from the Tower of Antonia. Alongside the public monuments there were a theater, a hippodrome, two profane swimming pools and a sacred one, the Sheep Pool, next to the Temple, which served for the washing of sacrificial victims. Then there were markets: the fish market to the east, the livestock and wood markets to the south, near the Temple, to which they supplied both burnt offerings and the fuel to burn them.

All these sites and buildings had in the course of centuries been destroyed and rebuilt and generally subjected to the vicissitudes of history. Twice conquered, by Joshua and David, before it definitely passed into Jewish hands and fell under the alternate rule of Judah and Israel, the city had already known glory and humiliation on so many occasions that to enumerate them would mean to recapitulate most of the Old Testament. The pillage of the Temple and the Royal Palace; the destruction of four hundred cubits of the walls by Joash, king of Israel, who subsequently returned to Samaria; the tribute of ten talents of gold and a hundred talents of silver claimed by Necho, king of Egypt, on his way back from an expedition to the Euphrates; the ravages of Nebuchadnezzar, king of Chaldea, who after his first attack led three thousand and twenty-three Jews into captivity in Babylon and then, during a fourth expedition, razed the Temple and indeed the whole city and made captives of the whole people and their king. Even before Nebuchadnezzar the city had changed hands nine times.

Nor was this the end of its vicissitudes. After the Babylonian captivity, around 500 B.C., Jerusalem was rebuilt and repeopled. But more destruction lay ahead. It was conquered by Alexander the Great and by several Egyptian kings. Ptolemy, son of Lagus, captured the city by wile and deported a hundred thousand of its inhabitants; Ptolemy Evergetes offered up sacrifices within its walls, Ptolemy Philopater was not allowed to enter the Temple and as a result exercised reprisals against the Jews in Egypt. The Seleucid dynasty of Syria was likewise involved in Jerusalem's history. Antiochus the Great exhibited his army and his elephants; he granted privileges to the Jews and gave money for sacrifices in the Temple. His son, Seleucus Philopater, was less generous, and indeed made inroads on the Temple's treasury. Seleucus Philopater's brother and successor, Antiochus Epiphanes, was received in Jerusalem with a torchlight procession and imagined himself to be popular among the Jews. Thirty years later, a false rumor of his death caused another and more genuine celebration, which roused him to such anger that he besieged the city, plundered it, took the gold and precious vessels out of the Temple and killed thousands of people. Two later kings of the same family, Antiochus Eupater and Antiochus Sidetes, destroyed Jerusalem's walls, but let Jewish kings rule over the defenseless city.

In the course of another one of the periods of turbulence, so common in the Middle East at this time, the high priest Hyrcanus called for help upon the Romans. Pompey captured Jerusalem and entered the sanctuary of the Temple, but as an ancient chronicler tells us, he "was so restrained that he touched none of the great treasures in this holy place. He admired the faithfulness of the priests, who had gone on with their worship amid the tumult and violence of the siege. On the day after he had taken over the Temple he commanded them to purify it and offer up sacrifices."

This was the beginning of Roman rule, which like any other occupation was alternately hostile and kindly. Augustus professed great respect for the Temple. He made gifts to it and ordered the daily sacrifice of an ox and two lambs on behalf of the Roman people. Pontius Pilate, on the other hand, was so scornful of Jewish customs that he started to make his entrance into the city under banners bearing the portrait of the deified Emperor, in defiance of the conquered people's aversion to "graven images." The Jews threw themselves onto the ground and declared that they were ready to die rather than suffer such a profanation. As a result, Pilate abandoned his plan. This episode, which took place fifteen years after Jesus' first visit to Jerusalem, shows how sensitive were the Jews to the holiness of their capital and its sanctuary and how prone were the Romans to make a display of their power.

As Jesus and his family approached the Holy City, the memory of its sieges and destruction, the profanations of the Temple and the alternate conflict and compromise between God and Caesar must have added a note of pathos to their awe.

Although Nazareth lies north of Jerusalem, Jesus and his family in all likelihood entered it from the south, in order not to cross the whole city to reach the Temple, a procedure frowned upon by the Roman police. After going through the Vale of Jehosaphat and crossing the Brook Kidron, they probably went in by the Gate of Siloam. This route held advantages for Romans and Jews alike. For the Romans because the crowd of pilgrims could be kept under watch from the Tower of Antonia; for the Jews because it led them by the Sheep Pool where they could, if they wished, prepare their sacrifices. Already from the Mount of Olives Jesus had seen the splendor of the Temple. At this time, probably in order to quiet his Jewish conscience, Herod was in the process of rebuilding and embellishing it. The reconstruction, begun in 19 B.C., was not yet finished when Jesus entered upon his ministry in A.D. 28.

Other things besides the Temple must have greeted his sight. All around the city of stone, a city of tents had been thrown up to house the faithful who had come to celebrate the Passover. The inaccurate Flavius Josephus would have us believe that the usual population of two hundred fifty thousand went up, at this season, to two and a half or three million. Let us, as some historians suggest, bring this extravagant figure down to a few hundred thousand. Even so, we can imagine that the young Jesus, fresh from the sparsely inhabited village of Nazareth, found himself in a crowd that must have seemed overwhelming. And that his eyes were dazzled by the city's architecture, particularly the gleaming gold and marble of the Temple.

And yet once he was over his initial surprise he may have felt a certain disappointment. Even on the Mount of Olives, the "hill of anointing," he could see the tables of the moneychangers and of the sellers of doves to be used as sacrifices, the inevitable hangers-on who in the vicinity of any sanctuary importune the faithful with their wares. Actually they were forbidden to enter the Temple. The

Talmud, which hands down the oral tradition of these times, tells us that the Temple was closed to "those who had money knotted into their handkerchiefs." Likewise, in the Berakhot, or tractate, we are told that no one could come with "canes or sacks or dirty feet." The Pharisees had strict laws against the changing of money or the display of sacrificial animals even in the courtyard of the Temple, and for this reason the merchants had installed themselves on the hill. Here, when he was only twelve years old, Jesus may have already felt the urge to chase them away. When Mary and Joseph saw how shocked he was by such crass commercialism, perhaps they quoted to him the words of the Talmud, which says: "The Temple is not to be made into a passageway." The influence of this precept is clearly to be seen in Mark's account of Jesus and the moneychangers, where it is said that he "would not suffer that any man should carry any vessel through the Temple." We may wonder, however, if this episode did not actually take place on the Mount of Olives rather than in the Temple, since within its precincts buying and selling were already forbidden.

Another thing that must have struck Jesus unfavorably was the presence of the Romans. Their soldiers did not merely keep watch over the city from the Tower of Antonia. A cordon of armed troops surrounded the walls and inspected everyone who went in. Moreover, the Roman governor, who lived during most of the year at Caesarea, came to Jerusalem for the three main Jewish religious festivals, particularly the Passover. Needless to say, this was not for any spiritual reason. The large numbers of Jews thronging the city were in a devotional mood that might easily take the form of a demonstration against the conqueror, and such a possibility demanded the presence of the emperor's highest representative and the embodiment of Roman law. Troops were stationed in the galleries near the Temple, not only to maintain order among the faithful but also as a reminder to the clergy of the fact that their tenure—even including that of the high priest—was subject to Roman approval.

The stolid Roman soldiers viewed with silent scorn the fervor of the more excitable Jews. According to the Roman historian Tacitus, whose understanding seems to have been on about the level of that of a centurion on guard in the streets of Jerusalem, Jewish customs were "base and abominable." As long as the Assyrians, Medes and Persians were masters of the region, Tacitus tells us, the Jews were considered "the meanest of their subjects." They were revolutionaries who refused to acknowledge the gods of Olympus or to feel any real allegiance to Rome. Strange to say, they believed that "the souls of those who are killed in battle or by the executioner are immortal." And this was only one of the alien features of the religion to which they were so devoted. "Moses introduced new religious practices, quite opposed to those of all other religions. The Jews regard as profane all that we hold sacred; on the other hand they permit all that we abhor . . . The Jews conceive of one god only, and that with the mind alone. They regard as impious those who make from perishable materials representations of gods in man's image; that supreme and eternal being is to them incapable of representation and without end. Therefore they set up no statues in their cities, still less in their temples; this flattery is not paid their kings, nor this honor given to the Caesars." Tacitus considered the Jews indolent because they rested every seventh day. And he added, misleadingly: "After a while they were led by the charms of indolence to give over the seventh year as well to inactivity."

And so, when the Passover pilgrims made their way to the Temple or pitched their city of tents under the scornful eyes of the Roman soldiery they must have been aware of the disparaging things that were being said about them. May not Jesus and his parents have overheard these remarks as well? When Jesus came down from the Mount of Olives and found himself under the watch of the Tower of Antonia, did he not become immediately aware of the clash between Israel and its proud pagan conquerors?

Still we may presume that his first impression was one of wonder at the Temple. The construction of this splendid and majestic building, the "navel of the universe," required, we are told, the labor of two hundred fifty thousand men over a period of eight years; it was 105 feet long, 37 feet wide and 52 feet high. The facade, which was the first thing to present itself to Jesus' sight, was in Greek rather than Hebrew style, flanked by two porches, one known for legendary reasons as "Solomon's Portico" (John 10:23; Acts 3:11; 5:12); the other as the "royal cloister," the latter composed of 162 Corinthian columns, set out in four rows and three aisles.

As he entered the building the young Jesus must have taken in its theological implications. At this time, when Israel possessed the only monotheistic religion, its wise men proceeded, scrupulously and yet broad-mindedly, to define its relationship to the pagan world. Tolerance and hierarchy were the practical aspects of their belief. They excluded no one from salvation, but involved everyone, including pagans and unbelievers, in humanity's march toward the advent of the Messiah. Israel has never held that infidels must be converted in order to have a place in God's plan. As the prophet Isaiah said: "My house shall be a house of prayer for all people."

But tolerance does not imply sloppiness or confusion. Respect for the moral law may suffice for the attainment of salvation, but it does not mean that all people are called upon to accomplish the same duties and the same religious mission. There is a gradation or hierarchy of privileges and duties. Israel is a land of priests, whose every thought and action are dedicated to the glory of God, but there are other categories of people, less strict in their observances, like the members of a "Third Order," who serve as intermediaries between Jews and idolaters. There are *gerim,* or proselytes, the *ger ha-sha-ar,* a proselyte "of the gate" who follows the Jewish rites only from a distance, but observes the moral law and the *ger-zaddik,* a "righteous" or more committed proselyte, who plays a greater part in the life of the community and accomplishes certain of its rites. And so all men and women who live as they should are drawn into the march toward salvation, taking their place, each according to his or her lights, around this people of priests, this people of Israel.

The Temple of Jerusalem had a layout that reflected this order of things. Between the Greek facade and the innermost sanctuary, devoid of ornaments and images, there was a series of "courts," accessible to various categories of people. There was the court of the Gentiles, open to foreigners and pagans, the court of Israel, with a section reserved for women, and finally the court of the priests. The Temple area was open to everybody; it was the spiritual center of the city and the nation.

Between the court of the Gentiles and the court of Israel there was a stone latticework with tablets forbidding the uncircumcised to pass within the sacred enclosures. The sanctuary itself was composed of three parts, indicative of various degrees of submission to God. First the "Vestibule," whose name is self-explanatory; then the "Holy" place; then the "Holy of Holies." The "Holy" place, separated from the "Vestibule" by four-colored curtains (symbolic of the four elements), was where the priests conducted worship and offered sacrifices; in it were the altar of perfumes or altar of gold, the seven-branched candlestick and the table for display of the unleavened showbread. The "Holy of Holies" contained the Ark of the Covenant, a chest two cubits and a half in length made of acacia wood, overlaid with gold, and topped by a gold lid, the "mercy-seat." The doors of the Holy of Holies were sealed; on only one day of the year, Yom Kippur or Day of Atonement, did the High Priest enter and accomplish a rite that is still described in the service of our own times:

> The faithful ones separated the High Priest one week before the tenth day . . . The water of purification was sprinkled upon him, and each day he sprinkled the blood, burned incense and trimmed the lamps that he might become accustomed to the sacred service . . .
>
> On the dawn of the ninth day they escorted him to the eastern gate, and some of the beautiful sacrifices of the Day of Atonement passed before him. Toward sunset the meal that was prepared for him was frugal, that his sleep might be calm; the aged men of his tribe led him forth to instruct him in taking his hands full of incense, and they charged him . . . to raise the pillar of incense within the Holy of Holies . . . He shed tears that his zeal should be doubted; they also shed tears; they sought . . . by expounding the Law and by reading Holy Writ to keep him wakeful until midnight . . . They to whom the first lot fell removed the ashes from the altar; the second lot was cast for the removal of the ashes from the altar of incense and from the lamp; the third lot . . . for one that should assist at the offering of incense; and for the arrangement of the members of the sacrifice was the fourth lot cast. As the watchman proclaimed the dawn of day, they spread a veil of fine linen to conceal him; he put off his clothes, bathed, and put on the golden garments; he stood and washed his hands and feet and performed the first part of the . . . morning . . . burnt offering. He appointed another to complete it; he then went to burn incense and to trim the lamps, to offer the burnt offering and to pour out a drink offering. Then spread they

again the linen veil; he then entered the chamber of Parvah, he washed his hands and feet and put off his golden garments. He went forth and bathed, and put on the white garments, and washed his hands and feet. These garments were made of fine linen from Pelusium, of the value of eighteen manim . . . fit for him that ministered unto the King of glory. The High Priest's bullock was placed between the porch and the altar, facing the west, with its head turned toward the south. He drew nigh unto it and, laying his hands upon its head, made confession of his transgressions, concealing naught in his bosom.

And thus did he say: "O GOD, I have sinned, I have committed iniquity, I have transgressed against thee, I and my household. I beseech you in your NAME, make atonement for the sins and for the iniquities and for the transgressions, where I have sinned and committed iniquity and transgressed against you, I and my household; as it is written in the Law of your servant Moses at your glorious command: For on this day atonement shall be made for you, to cleanse you; from all your sins, before the LORD."

And when the priests and the people that stood in the court heard the glorious and awful Name pronounced out of the mouth of the High Priest in holiness and in purity, they knelt and prostrated themselves . . . saying: "Blessed be his glorious, sovereign NAME for ever and ever."

And he, in awe, prolonged the utterance of the Name, until they that said the blessing had ended it; to whom he said: "You shall be clean."

We may imagine then that on the tenth day of the month of Tishri, the Day of Atonement, four or five hundred thousand people from all over the country stood outside the Temple while twenty thousand priests, divided into twenty-four watches, officiated within. The thoughts of all of them were with the High Priest as, on this one day of the year, he stood alone before God and trembling pronounced God's name.

As the Passover pilgrims, mindful of the Atonement ceremonial, walked through the successive courts of the Temple, each of them one remove farther from the world of men and women and closer to God, they must have felt a deepening awe and reverence although, as we shall see, they only imperfectly succeeded in banishing all profane thoughts from their minds.

Certainly after the village synagogue to which he was accustomed, Jesus must have found the size of the Temple, "the visible expression of a whole people's faith," overwhelming. The Temple was the center of both national and religious life; in both Exodus (23:17) and Deuteronomy (16:16) the Jews were ordered to appear before God in a place of God's choosing three times a year. In the month of Adar, just before the Passover, every Jew except the priests had to pay to the Temple a *didrachmon*, or half a silver shekel, of tribute money. At Jesus' time the doctors were still discussing at what age children should attend its functions.

Worship in the Temple had none of the intimate or educational character of that of the synagogue. It consisted primarily of sacrifice, and there were no provisions for the teaching of the Law. According to the *midrashim,* the Temple was half earthly, half heavenly in nature; it was at the meeting point of two horizons, one immanent, one transcendent. The Temple of Jerusalem, the Temple built in Eretz Israel, on the rocky, muddy, earthy "promised land," was a counterpart of the inaccessible sanctuary that the Messiah might be on the point of approaching. According to the second-century Rabbi Simeon ben Johai, when a perfect monument is built here on earth it is re-created in heaven.

The splendor of the Temple, the crowds inside and around it, the majestic character of its sacrifices and the otherworldliness of its worship could not fail to impress pilgrims from the provinces, the young Jesus of Nazareth among them. But for Israel there can be no uplift without downfall, no exultation untinged by regret. This is perhaps the consequence of its fundamental paradox, its earthly incarnation of a divinely inspired destiny. This magnificent edifice, consecrated to the highest purpose conceived by people, was made of gross stone and by human hands, with all their connotations of impurity.

To Israel there was already something scandalous about building in space. The Jews' vocation is to build in time; their true temples are in the human heart and part of history, never finished and indeed owing their endurance to this very incompleteness. They convey tradition without either freezing or interrupting it, without coinciding and perishing with a single one of time's fleeting moments. Jewry's true monuments, as we shall see later on, are continuous commentaries of the word of God.

The origin of the Temple, this magnificent edifice, which at the same time expresses and consolidates Israel's love for the Creator in a way contrary to the earliest tradition, goes back to the crucial episode of the worship of the Calf of Gold. It was after this idolatry and in order to prevent its recurrence that the Children of Israel were ordered to make a tabernacle and build a temple to house it. The *midrash* states this clearly: "Lord of the world, earthly kings have palaces, where there are tables and candlesticks and other symbols which make for recognition of their royal status. And you, our liberator and savior, would you not have some sign of royalty, so that all the inhabitants of earth may recognize you as King?"

When Solomon finally built this spatial dwelling, so little in keeping with the essential infinity of God, he had to overcome all sorts of resistance. First, the resistance of people, for he had to call upon non-Jewish, Phoenician workers. And second, what we may call the resistance of God, that is, if we explore the meaning of the strange verse of 2 Chronicles (6:18): "But will God indeed reside with mortals on earth? Even heaven and the highest heaven cannot contain you, how much less this house that I have built!"

This hesitation or scrupulosity on God's part has left its mark on the conscience of Israel. There is no certainty that the Unspeakable, Invisible, Elusive One, in spite of all the precautions with which the liturgy hedged him about, was truly at ease in the Temple. Flavius Josephus (*The Jewish War*, VI, 299), corroborated by Tacitus (V, 13), recounts a surprising incident in this connection. A few years before the destruction of the Temple by fire, "At the feast of Pentecost, when the priests had gone into the Inner Temple at night to perform the usual ceremonies, they declared that they were aware, first of a violent movement and a loud crash, then of a concerted cry: 'Let us go hence!' The voice was that of the God of Israel, who refused to let himself be enclosed in stone walls."

The very fact of construction, of an attempt to isolate a unit of the immense space created by God and thus to check the flow of time, was to the Jew of this period shocking and almost idolatrous. Is there not a connection here with the punishment that God brought down upon the builders of the Tower of Babel? A well-known *midrash* furnishes us this explanation. During the construction of the Tower a man fell from the scaffolding and was killed. The builders were so obsessed by their desire to finish this monument to their fame that they ordered the body to be taken away without a pause in the work. A few days later a segment of the wall crumbled, and the consequent disruption of their schedule and loss of money disturbed them far more than the death of one of their workers. Perhaps this was the reason why God visited such a dramatic punishment upon them.

This is an unusual case, but the fact remains that all Jews are ill at ease when it comes to consecrating a finite building to the infinite God. The Torah bears out their fear, for in Exodus (20:25) God says to Moses: "But if you make for me an altar of stone, do not build it of hewn stones; for if you use a chisel upon it you profane it."

The gleaming white stones with which Herod the Great had ornamented the Temple, no matter how they may have dazzled the young Jesus' eyes, had been hewn by human hands and thereby subjected to profanation. The rebuilt sanctuary, in spite of its splendor, the vicissitudes through which it had lived and the people's attachment to it, aroused mingled feelings among them. The elaborate monument probably shocked rather than pleased those Israelites who cherished the simple traditions of the original cult of Jehovah. Magnificent in gold and cedar, Herod's ornamentation of the Temple must have seemed to them an attempt to blend their faith, symbolized by the Ark of the Covenant, with various foreign cults, particularly those of the Phoenicians. For the colonnades and the outer decorations of the Temple were certainly not Jewish in character.

It is difficult to imagine the complex feelings of the young boy of Nazareth when he made this first pilgrimage to Jerusalem. In his village he had been accustomed, every month, to see fires lit on the surrounding hills to announce the coming of the new moon, and he knew that this signal was one link in a chain originated on the Mount of Olives by the priests of the Temple. Until his thirteenth year and this visit to the capital, these fires had been the chief bond to the sanctuary. The Temple had been not only the center of the world, the earthly habitation of the historical God; it was also, visibly, the center of light, the determinant of the calendar.

And when he finally arrived in this place of mystery he found it guarded by Roman soldiers, surrounded by merchants and decked with foreign ornamentation. What a shock to his youthfully ingenuous sensitivity! What bitterness there must have been in his heart! Such a traumatic experience must have played a large part in his spiritual evolution.

CHAPTER SIX

The Young Jesus among the Doctors

THE HOLIDAY CROWD MILLING through the city streets and the courts of the Temple was not composed only of believers. Every religion numbers people who pay little heed—except on special occasions—to its ordinances: Jews who feel obliged to fast on Yom Kippur in order to join in the prayer for the dead; Christians who observe Good Friday and Easter, even if they do not set foot in church during the rest of the year. In Jerusalem, where the circumstances of the occupation caused Romans, Greeks and Jews to find themselves together, there were, then, atheists, skeptics and violators of the law. In this last category were *avaryanim*, or "sinners," who were either unable or unwilling to repent; "publicans," or tax-collectors, who were regarded as depraved because they profited in the service of Rome; and petty artisans, servants and farm laborers, who rarely visited Jerusalem or paid attention to the doctrines of their faith.

During the Passover celebration such lost sheep must have passed by or even entered the Temple, where they heard the echo of prayers, which they had long since forgotten or even imagined that, by their passive presence, they were taking part in the out-pourings of the faithful. It was among a motley crowd of this description that Mary and Joseph must have led Jesus as they made their way to the vicinity of the sanctuary. Here also that they looked for him, at first in vain, and then, after three days found him "sitting in the midst of the doctors, both hearing them, and asking them questions."

When the young Jesus came for the first time since he was a baby to the Temple he passed through this crowd of tepid believers, but he did not linger among them. The doctors welcomed him as a boy preparing for his bar mitzvah or religious initiation. To this custom there is an important and almost contemporary witness. The Hellenized Jewish historian, Flavius Josephus, who was born a short time after Jesus' death, tells in his autobiography that when he himself was sixteen years old he started to explore the spiritual currents of his time. He studied the opinions of the three principal Jewish sects, the Pharisees, the Sadducees and the Essenes (he makes no mention of the overeager Zealots), in order, as he says, "that I should be in a position to select the best." Even before this, at the time of his religious initiation, he tells us, "the chief priests and leading men of the city used constantly to come to me for pre-cise information on some particular in our ordinances."

We may conclude that at Jesus' time the doctors welcomed any boy of his age, either to test his knowledge or to let him share one of the incessant dialogues about the Law, so essential a part of the Jewish religion, in which he was not a mere listener but was enti-tled to express an opinion. The doctors were not dictatorial dog-matists but guides and partners in the "open forum" of rabbinical tradition.

But exactly who were these doctors? Did they belong to the same sect as those who questioned Flavius Josephus, twenty-five years later? Probably not, for the two boys were of very different origins. Flavius Josephus was an aristocrat, and proud of it; among his ancestors there were high priests and kings, and his father was known all over Jerusalem for his noble lineage and his love of justice. He himself had no need to work for a living. In leisurely fashion he completed his studies, examined the possibilities of finding something to interest him in Jerusalem, then lived for three years, with a certain Bannos, "who dwelt in the wilderness, wearing only such clothing as trees provided, feeding on such things as grew of themselves and using frequent ablutions of cold water, by day and night, for purity's sake." After this voluntary taste of asceticism Flavius Josephus returned to everyday life and at twenty-six years of age, in the course of a trip to Rome, was introduced to the Emperor Nero's wife, Poppaea.

A boy so well-born and well-connected would not have been received in the Temple in the same everyday way as Jesus. The "chief priests and leading men" to whom he refers were doubtless Sadducees. By birth and rank he was entitled to their favor. Young Jesus of Nazareth, on the other hand, would have held no interest for them whatsoever. They would have been too busy with the Passover rites and sacrifices to receive him.

Jesus, as we know, came before doctors skilled in the knowledge and dialectic of the Law and endowed with a rich spiritual life but not with a high social standing. In accord with the rabbinical tradition, he was to address himself particularly to the poor and humble. Meanwhile we may wonder who were these doctors who found time during the Passover celebration to question and answer an unknown young boy, to deepen his understanding of the religion of Israel and to awaken in him, perhaps, a consciousness of his mission. To what sect did they belong?

The sects of Jesus' time were spiritual parties within the framework of Judaism. They all had the same dogma, worship and historical tradition, and differed only in the emphasis they placed upon certain external manifestations of their common faith. The two sects that differed most in their practices were the Zealots, who were highly organized and went in for political action, and the Essenes, who were the most spiritual and cultivated contemplation. To neither one of these is it likely that the doctors who received Jesus in the Temple belonged.

The Zealots believed in bringing about the Messianic age by force; they were fanatical nationalists who did not hesitate to mingle piety with violence. The other sects, particularly the Pharisees, believed in the advent of the Messiah, but their belief was a pious hope rather than a call to action. They looked for Israel's deliverance in the strict observation of the Law; obedience to the commandments and the accomplishment of the prescribed prayers and ceremonies were the only steps they took to bring about the Kingdom of Heaven. The Pharisees were mystics and intellectuals, and the Zealots must have branded them as ineffective. A hundred years after Jesus' death, in their attempt to force God's hand, the Zealots fostered a Messianic king, Simeon Bar-Kokhba, who had only one Pharisee, Rabbi Akiba, for a supporter. No Zealots, then, would have received Jesus in the Temple at Jerusalem, whose clergy was, if not designated, at least accepted and watched over by the Romans.

For opposite reasons it is unlikely that the doctors belonged to the contemplative sect of the Essenes, who had shut themselves off from their countrymen and the capital city and withdrawn to primitive monasteries on the west shore of the Dead Sea. Although their beliefs, including that in the immortality of the soul, were similar to those of the Pharisees, their way of life was entirely different. They formed a sort of secret society whose rites were open only to initiates.

There remain, then, the Sadducees and the Pharisees, both of whom might have been present in the Temple during the holy days and have received a newcomer. But their attitudes were not at all the same. The Sadducees disapproved of nonconformity in politics, philosophy or religion. Politically, they adapted themselves successfully to the Roman occupation and even to the interference with Temple affairs. Although Herod had conferred the priesthood upon nomads from outside Palestine who were the docile instruments of his will and had filled forced vacancies on the Sanhedrin with priests imported from Alexandria, the Sadducees did not hesitate to worship beside them. They did not look down upon the language and culture of the Greeks which, according to Flavius Josephus, most Jews of Jesus' time considered as suited only to slaves. The Talmud forbade speaking Greek, and those who spoke it automatically cut themselves off from the faith. Besides, a good Jew had no time for such study. A Pharisee, tempted by modernism, is said to have asked a rabbi whether his son could learn Greek. And the rabbi answered: "Why not? But our sages recommend spending all day and all night in the study of the Torah. Try to find an hour which belongs neither to night nor to day."

The Sadducees, having adapted themselves to the civilization of the conquerors, did not hesitate to learn Greek or Latin. But when it came to religion they held out for the naked text of the Scriptures and refused to admit the tradition of exegesis and interpretation. The Pharisees, on the contrary, proclaimed themselves to be nonconformists. Their Hebrew name is *Perushim*, which means "the separated ones," separated from the higher-ups of either government or clergy. They were of pure Jewish, lower-class origin and infused with a liberal spirit; instead of keeping to the letter of the Law they were the initiators of the rabbinical commentaries, both Talmud and *midrashim*. Since they were unprejudiced and at the same time patriotic, they did not boycott the national and religious institution of the Temple, but preferred the more easygoing and democratic synagogue, which was indeed their contribution to Judaism. It seems likely that they gathered in the synagogue which, as we have said above, formed within the Temple itself an island of simple, unofficial piety, and it is here that they may very well have received Jesus.

We cannot say that the doctors mentioned in the Gospel according to Luke included no Sadducees, but we can be reasonably sure that Pharisees constituted the majority among them. First, on the supposition that we have hazarded above, that they were the group most likely to receive a mere carpenter's son. And second, because of the echoes of their doctrine, which we find in Jesus' own teaching. In spite of the fact that Jesus' disciples frequently clashed with the Pharisees, they had an obvious influence upon him. As we shall see later, many sentences in the Talmud are to be found in the Gospels.

Toward the Romans the Pharisees' attitude was one of compromise; they refused either to serve or to combat them. This position is close to that which Jesus expressed in his famous saying: "Render therefore unto Caesar the things which are Caesar's . . ." Flavius Josephus' comparison between the Sadducees and the Pharisees gives further evidence of the relationship of the latters' doctrine to the preaching of Jesus:

> *The Pharisees, are held to be the most authoritative exponents of the Law . . . They ascribe everything to Fate or to God: the decision whether or not to do right rests mainly with men, but in every action Fate takes some part. Every soul is incorruptible, but only the souls of good men pass into other bodies, the souls of bad men being subjected to eternal punishment.*

(On this last point, that of eternal punishment, Flavius Josephus has, as we shall see, misinterpreted the rabbis.)

The doctors, whom we may identify, along general lines, with the Pharisees, in their attitude toward the Romans, the priestly clan and the political activists, exercised their influence from the Temple synagogue, which they had made into a center of religious purity and intellectual freedom. It was doubtless among them that Jesus spent the three days when his parents could not find him, discussing the Scriptures and their rabbinical comments.

How, then, did this early affinity turn into dissension, until the name of Pharisee, which Jesus respected when he was a boy, became an object of scorn for him and his disciples? Was it by virtue of a misunderstanding or as the result of a process of natural and logical evolution? In order to resolve this enigma we must examine more closely the behavior of the Pharisees in Jesus' time.

There were Pharisees and Pharisees, and the discredit into which the whole sect fell was probably due to a minority of its followers. At just this time, the beginning of the Christian era, the Pharisees, in a self-critical mood, differentiated in the Talmud between the good and the bad among their number. With often biting humor they listed seven categories, to six of which they gave picturesque nicknames that justified their bad reputation.

There are, the Talmud says, seven kinds of Pharisees:

1. The "Broad-shouldered," who carry their religious duties on their backs, ostentatiously;

2. The "Stumblers," who with excessive humility knock their feet together;

3. The "Head-bangers," who look down at the ground in order not to see passing women and bang their heads against a wall;

4. The "Pestles," who bend over double as they walk;

5. Those that say: "Tell me what is my duty, so I may go
and perform it";
   6. Those that do good out of fear;
   7. Those that do good out of love.

We can imagine how a Rabelais, a Molière or even a Pascal might savor the caustic quality of the description of the first six categories. Among the good Pharisees of the time there were those who anticipated the judgment passed by the Talmud and denounced their unworthy fellows. Rabbi Nachman says: "The High Court will punish those hypocrites who wrap themselves up in their prayer shawls in order to pose as true Pharisees, when they are nothing of the sort." Another adversary of the sect, Alexander Jannaeus, said, when dying, to his wife: "Have no fear of true Pharisees or of those who are not Pharisees at all, but be careful of 'painted Pharisees,' who are pretending to be what they are not."

The fact that this "painting," or pretense, was spread unequally through the sect is shown not only by Jewish texts but by Christian ones as well. If we look carefully at the Gospels we shall see that they make the same distinction between "good" Pharisees and "bad" ones. We find, of course, the appellation "generation of vipers" and many more, but other Gospel passages show us Pharisees of a deserving kind. Luke (13:31–33) for instance, pays tribute to those who sought to protect Jesus from the wrath of Herod:

At that very hour some Pharisees came and said to him,
"Get away from here, for Herod wants to kill you."
   He said to them, "Go and tell that fox for me, 'Listen, I am
casting out demons and performing cures today and tomorrow, and
on the third day I finish my work. Yet today, tomorrow, and the
next day I must be on my way, because it is impossible for a
prophet to be killed outside of Jerusalem.'"

The Pharisees' good intentions bore no fruit, but it is notewor-thy that they rose to defend Christ against the king who was a notorious collaborator of the pagans. And in the Acts of the Apostles we find two episodes in which the Pharisees are cast in a favorable light. First, when the Sanhedrin had gathered together to condemn the apostles (5:34–39):

> *But a Pharisee named Gamaliel, a teacher of the law, respect-ed by all the people, stood up and ordered the men to be put out-side for a short time.*
>
> *Then he said to them [of the Sanhedrin], "Fellow Israelites, consider carefully what you propose to do to these men.*
>
> *For some time ago Theudas rose up, claiming to be somebody, and a number of men, about four hundred, joined him; but he was killed, and all, who followed him were dispersed and disappeared.*
>
> *After him Judas the Galilean rose up at the time of the census and got people to follow him; he also perished, and all who fol-lowed him were scattered.*
>
> *So in the present case, I tell you, keep away from these men and let them alone; because if this plan or this undertaking is of human origin, it will fail;*
>
> *But if this is of God, you will not be able to overthrow them—in that case you may even be found fighting against God!"*
>
> *They were convinced by him . . .*

After this scene, where spirituality wins out over legalism, the Acts of the Apostles show us Saint Paul before the Sanhedrin, where the Pharisees take his side, and he distinguishes them from the Sadducees and professes to belong to their number (23:6–10):

> *When Paul noticed that some were Sadducees and others were Pharisees, he called out in the council, "Brothers, I am a Pharisee, a son of Pharisees. I am on trial concerning the hope of the resur-rection of the dead."*

> *When he said this, a dissension began between the Pharisees*
> *and the Sadducees, and the assembly was divided.*
>
> *(The Sadducees say that there is no resurrection, or angel, or*
> *spirit; but the Pharisees acknowledge all three.)*
>
> *Then a great clamor arose, and certain scribes of the Pharisees'*
> *group stood up and contended, "We find nothing wrong with this*
> *man. What if a spirit or an angel has spoken to him?"*
>
> *When the dissension became violent, the tribune, fearing that*
> *they would tear Paul to pieces, ordered the soldiers to go down,*
> *take him by force, and bring him into the barracks.*

And so the Talmud on the one hand and Luke and Acts on the other, no matter how diversely they judge the Pharisees, agree not to put them all in the same category. The Talmud praises those who were faithful to their religion, one category out of seven, but perhaps the most numerous and certainly the most representative. The New Testament, naturally, is indulgent toward those who seem to be forerunners of allies of Christianity. Perhaps the same spiritual values were involved, with different applications, or perhaps there was not then the chasm between Judaism and Christianity that has come into being through centuries of debate and persecution. In any case the Pharisees, or certain ones among them, represented the best and most generous of Jewish traditions, although under particular historical circumstances their very virtues lent themselves to dislike. How did it happen that the Pharisees won such praise, only to become the objects of misunderstanding?

The Pharisees stood for all that was liberal and at the same time for all that was uncompromising in the Jewish religion of their time. To a modern mind these two terms may seem contradictory, but this was not the case in the religious atmosphere of two thousand years ago.

To the Pharisees a revealed text, although it could not be tampered with, was nevertheless subject to commentary and explanation. We have only to recall the *midrash,* which shows Moses on Mount Sinai receiving God's law and at the same time looking into the future and seeing all the commentaries that will be made upon it, many of them stemming from civilizations he cannot conceive and phrased in languages he does not know. Yet he gives full powers to his remotest descendants and declares himself in accord with the future reverberations of his word, even if they are incomprehensible to him. In consenting to interpretations at whose spirit he could guess but whose literal meaning must escape him, Moses was acting like a Pharisee.

At the same time the Pharisees were in a way, literally, the first freethinkers. But at a period when the whole universe still had a sacred character their freethinking was bound up with their religion; it was made manifest not in denial of the faith but in commentaries that elaborated upon it. This is the origin of those two monuments of Judaism, the Talmud and the *midrash.* The Pharisees engaged ceaselessly in the exegesis of the Torah. They would not allow it to be monopolized by the priests, but adapted it to the social and individual needs of those ordinary yet extraordinary creatures, women and men, subject to eternity, yet living in history. In so doing they multiplied the applications of God's law.

The philosophy of the Pharisees was human not only in its origins but in its consequences as well. They were all gentleness and charity toward their fellow human beings, ceaselessly preaching that people must love their neighbor like themselves. In their view there was no sin that could not be forgiven, no eternal punishment. When the Talmud takes up the question of punishments in the next world it limits their duration and proportions as nearly as possible to the gravity of the sin, as if on the part of some earthly tribunal. The maximum term is one year. Pharisee sages always set forth the possibility of divine pardon. They taught that God was merciful toward a sincerely repentant sinner, not out of weakness but out of understanding of the true nature of mercy. For the essence of repentance and forgiveness is not simply the cancellation of a debt; it is the renewal of personal relations between the soul and God, of the harmony that sin has broken.

This human and generous conception of the relations between God and humans was paralleled by one equally broad of the relations between one person and another. Pharisaic morality was deeply committed to freedom, in the most enduring and modern sense of the word; one might call it close to the "personalism" of today. It affirmed the primacy of every man and women in their double reality, individual and communal. Each person was not to be submitted to the arithmetical laws by which there is superiority in numbers and a majority decision obliterates private opinion. Every soul was autonomous, every mind independent.

The Mishnah, that first written expression of oral rabbinical tradition, states the reason why no opinion, however isolated, can be overlooked. It is "in order that, if circumstances make it necessary, a court can use it as the basis of support of a judgment." Hillel, who, as we shall see later on, represented the best qualities of the Pharisees and antedated those of the Christians, came out with a precept inimical to hasty and preconceived notions of justice: "Do not judge your neighbor until you have been in the same situation as he." The Pharisee doctors pushed freedom of opinion as far as it could go. No idea could be more truly revolutionary than this one of a Pharisee rabbi: "Disobedience to a precept with the intention of serving God is better than obedience without any such intention." Where, in all this, is the narrow ritualism habitually attributed to the Pharisees?

Their respect for individual freedom was incarnated in a communal institution particularly suited to their temperament, the synagogue, a house of prayer where any one of the faithful could conduct the service and interpret the law, as did Jesus, Saint Paul and the first Christians.

The Synagogue and the Talmud were, then, the framework and the written expression of the Pharisees' love of freedom. It has been said of the Talmud that it kept the spirit of Israel alive when the people themselves were prevented from carrying out their historical mission In the same way the synagogues were spiritual refuges and sanctuaries, where the Pharisees maintained the traditions of liberty and justice. And yet, by a paradox that the modern mind may find unnecessarily difficult to accept, these Pharisees who were the most liberal of the Jews of their time were also the most strict in their religious observances.

To the Pharisees, every Jew, as a result of the Covenant, was a priest and the whole world had a sacred character. "You shall be to me a kingdom of priests, and an holy nation," says one of the most moving verses of Exodus. Of course, ever since the Creation, humans had been bound to the universe in which God was manifested. Hence the importance of every word, every letter of the Scriptures, which lend themselves to infinite commentary, since in them the Eternal God is shown forth, at all times and in all places. Hence also the importance of every human action, which has power to either strengthen or weaken the harmony of the universe, the weightiness of every commandment and the culpability of every error in its interpretation.

In this sacred universe, where every word expresses God and every gesture may serve to carry out God's will, every sentence, every action has a significance almost like that of the liturgy of the Catholic Mass or the motions of the priest during its celebration.

But whereas, for the Christian, this sanctification of word and deed culminates in the mystery of the Mass, for the Jew there is no one culminating point. At every moment of their life, in every place of their earthly pilgrimage, Jews belong to a sacred universe of which they are both the witness and the priest. Hence the importance of the detailed study of the Torah and its application. (As Monsignor Ricciotti has put it: "It was from tradition that the Pharisees derived the doctrines which the Sadducees had rejected. Since the study of the Law, particularly the oral Law, was the Jew's most stringent duty and noblest occupation they dedicated their whole time to it.")

They had been told also that "the study of the Torah is something greater than the building of the Temple . . . or the veneration for a father or mother" (Megillah 16 b), that "a man must not abandon the house of study (of the Law) even at the hour of his death" (Shabbat 13 b).

Here we have the reason for the high standards of the Pharisees. Where there was true belief in the sacred character of the world and the ministry of human kind, these standards had a compelling necessity about them. But where, on the other hand, Pharisees had lost their faith and simply went through its motions, the result was an empty ritualism. There was an immense number of Pharisee prescriptions, six hundred thirteen in all, three hundred sixty-five (as many as the days of the year) negative and two hundred forty-eight (as many as the muscles of the human body) positive. Their general purpose was to keep people faithful to the Covenant, and the thousand links of this network had some reason for being as long as they enclosed something of a universe, which was looked upon as divine.

But when, under Roman influence, the Jewish world began to lose its sacred character and the Jewish religion, heretofore pure,

turned to idolatry, then the spontaneity and sincerity of the Pharisees started to become arbitrary and artificial. A change of this kind
was in the air, perceptible to Jewish society as a whole and to the
most sensitive of the Pharisees in particular, in Jesus' time.

This, perhaps, was the basis of the misunderstanding to which
the Pharisees lent themselves, the reason for the divergence
between Jesus and some of their number. A divergence that no one
could have foreseen and for which neither party was really responsible, since the real responsibility lies with the Romans, whose
presence around the Temple and interference in Jewish religious
life had broken the sacred harmony of the world in which Jesus
had been brought up, the world in which Israel had played out its
destiny for two thousand years.

The presence of Roman paganism and rationalism at the very
gates of the sanctuary so transformed the atmosphere in which the
Pharisees were engaged in following and elaborating the word of
God that it made their whole way of life seem paralyzed and
anachronistic. If Jesus, in the course of his preaching, broke away
from the Pharisees and his disciples disputed with them, the fault
was that of the centurion who on holy days mounted guard over the
sanctuary, of Herod, who submitted the list of the Temple clergy to
Roman approval of the Hellenized Jews who, thinking that God
could be reconciled with Caesar, had insinuated themselves into all
the courts of the Temple, those reserved for Jews and non-Jews alike.

True Pharisees were aware of the threat that the occupation
forces represented to the religion of Israel. One of them took refuge
in a cave in order to escape the profane world of the conquerors.
"He was repulsed by the calculating and utilitarian spirit of Roman
civilization."

When the twelve-year-old Jesus lingered for three days with
the doctors, probably in the synagogue of the Temple, things had

not yet come to this pass. The conflict that was to set him and his disciples against the Pharisees had not yet consciously developed. Yet the young Nazarene must have found the atmosphere of the Temple different from that of the house of prayer to which he was accustomed in his native place. There were some resemblances to be sure, which made the Temple synagogue not entirely unfamiliar to him. For one thing it was surrounded by study rooms, to which Jesus, as a candidate for bar mitzvah, was automatically admitted. The blessings sung during the services were those he already knew, and the doctors, when they were at their devotions, wore the same prayer shawl as Joseph, or the rabbi of Nazareth, or the *hazzan*, the cantor, who had perhaps taught Jesus the rudiments of the Law.

But outside this familiar framework Jerusalem teamed with a whole world of things Jesus did not know. Everywhere the Romans made a show of their power. And the talk he heard around him was not all in the familiar Aramaic tongue; it was also in Hebrew, the language of the intellectuals, and in Greek and Latin, as spoken by the pagan conquerors.

It would be impossible or at the very least ill-advised, in speaking of this critical episode of the hidden years, to reconstruct what Jesus said to the doctors which, according to Luke, so greatly astonished them. We can reconstruct with greater accuracy what the doctors said to him, or rather the sort of thing they were saying at this period. There are sayings, known to be of the contemporary Pharisees, which were in the air, in the air of this time, pregnant with the future, when Jesus made the first public showing of his vocation.

The doctors, many of them, had qualities he could not have failed to appreciate. We have seen that they affirmed the primacy of the spirit in the face of Roman materialism; we have seen that they were liberal and indulgent, that they proclaimed and applied

the law of love. Most of them were also aware of Jewish universalism and refused to exclude other peoples and religions from the
salvation to be brought to earth by the coming of God's kingdom.
"Is it not noteworthy," writes Rabbi Elie Benamozegh, the nineteenth-century Jewish thinker, "that in the days of Caligula, Ti-
berius and Nero the Pharisees should have debated the question of
whether a pagan, faithful to his own religion, could be saved as
long as he confessed the Creator and led a good life? And over the
centuries this broad, affirmative doctrine has prevailed, so that
today every Jew must believe that Marcus Aurelius occupies just as
much of a place in Paradise as Isaac and Moses." Indeed, the Pharisees went so far as to say that a good pagan might be the equal or
even the superior of the high priest of Jerusalem.

This broad-mindedness did not reflect a lukewarm faith. The
very Pharisees who offered to share Israelis prerogatives with other
peoples were ready to die heroically for their beliefs. Less than ten
years after the Crucifixion large numbers of Jews boldly faced a
martyr's death when the Emperor Caligula tried to place a statue of
himself in the Temple of Jerusalem. Thousands of Jews prostrated
themselves before Petronius, the Roman envoy encamped with his
army on the plain of Acre. With humility and courage, they demanded that he either refrain from putting the statue in the
Temple or else kill them all.

Among these thousands of Jews, faithful at the price of their
life to the Torah, may not there have been some who had received
their religious instruction from the same doctors as Jesus? Surely
we cannot dismiss the Pharisees as mere narrow ritualists. Among
the doctors there must have been a spiritual atmosphere such as to
stimulate the young Jesus' Messianic vocation.

At the same time the doctors carried on minute analysis and
discussion, which were responsible for both the vitality and the

danger of paralysis inherent in the Pharisees' religion. When Jesus came to the Temple there were two rival schools of thought: those of Hillel and Shammai, both of whom died at just about this date. Hillel the Elder, or the Great, was the head of an academy that existed in Jerusalem between 40 B.C. and A.D. 10. In opposition to this *Bet* (House of) *Hillel* there was the *Bet Shammai*, which represented a divergent branch of Pharisaic doctrine. When Jesus met the doctors, the memory of these two schools was still fresh, and disciples continued to spread their teachings. But whatever their divergences, Hillel and Shammai both represented the Talmudic tradition, which goes all the way back to Moses. This is how the Pirke Abot presents their common genealogy:

> *Moses received the Torah on Sinai and handed it down to Joshua; Joshua gave it to the elders; the elders to the prophets; and the prophets handed it down to the men of the Great Assembly. They said three things: Be deliberate in judgment; raise up many disciples; and build a fence around the Torah . . .*
>
> *Shemaya and Abtalyon received the tradition. . . The former said: "Love work, hate domination, and seek no undue intimacy with the ruling power." The latter said: "You sages be heedful of your words, lest your disciples be misled and the name of Heaven be profaned."*
>
> *Hillel and Shammai received the tradition from them . . .*
> *(Pirke Abot, 1–12).*

Coming from the same line and nourished by the same sources the two doctors brought different temperaments to their doctrinal interpretations. Both of them, faithful to Pharisaic philosophy, tried to formulate it in a kindly and indulgent manner. Of Hillel's teaching we have many examples, which we shall quote below. Shammai has been too often described as his complete opposite; it is unjust to consider him for this reason narrow and sectarian. Here is how the Pirke Abot quotes him: "Set a fixed time for the study of the Torah; say little and do much; and receive all men with a cheerful countenance."

But according to later writers, and perhaps his contemporaries as well, there were behind Shammai's smiling face a doctrinal rigor and concern with detail greater than those of any other doctor. History is given to oversimplification, and if Hillel is reputed to have been a liberal and Shammai a ritualist, it may be upon the evidence of writings chosen, in both cases, to support an a priori idea.

According to the Talmud, Shammai was intransigent even toward his own family. He wanted his son, at a tender age, to fast on the day of Yom Kippur. Later, when his daughter-in-law gave birth to a child during the feast of Tabernacles, he removed the ceiling from the room and replaced it with branches, in order that his newborn grandson should accomplish his religious duty in the leafy "booths," or tents, prescribed by Leviticus.

Hillel, on the other hand, is said to have interpreted the Law in a much more generous fashion. Hence the pupils and later followers of the two doctors were in almost constant disagreement. They disagreed, for instance, on the age at which children were to be brought to the Temple. The rabbis of the School of Shammai maintained that it should be as soon as they were able to sit astride their fathers' shoulders, whereas the followers of Hillel put it off until they were able to walk up the steps, holding their fathers' hands.

Another, even more characteristic discussion revolved around the conditions of admission to the two schools. According to a *baraita,* or note added to the Talmud, the pupils of Shammai were required to be "modest, intelligent, well-born and rich," whereas those of Hillel had to meet no regular requirements whatsoever, because "many sinners, once they had been instructed in the Law, became good, religious men."

The differences between the two schools, we repeat, were not in the interpretation of tradition, but simply in the characters of their leaders. This is made clear by a Talmudic story about a pagan who came asking to be instructed in the Law.

> *A pagan came to Shammai and said: "I'm willing to become a Jew, but you must teach me the whole of the Law while I am standing on one foot." Shammai rapped his knuckles with a ruler and sent him away. The would-be convert then went to Hillel, who told him: "Do not unto others what you would not they do unto you. That is the whole of the Law; the rest is only commentary. Go, and learn this" (Shabbat 30 a).*

Hillel's reply bears a striking resemblance to that which Jesus made, according to the Gospel of Mark (12:28–31), under very similar circumstances:

> *One of the scribes came near and heard them disputing with one another, and seeing that he answered them well, he asked him, "Which Commandment is the first of all?"*
>
> *Jesus answered, "The first is, 'Hear, O Israel: the Lord our God, the Lord is one; you shall love the Lord your God with all your heart, and with all your soul, and with all your mind, and with all your strength.'*
>
> *The second is this, 'You shall love your neighbor as yourself.' There is no other commandment greater than these."*

It seems then that when the young Jesus came to the Temple the first question in his mind must have been not whether he should accept the teaching of the Pharisees, but rather how he should choose from the various degrees of rigor among them. The

Jewish thought of his time was much concerned with this problem. The Talmud says:

> For three years the schools of Hillel and Shammai disputed together, each one saying: "My word is the Law." Then a voice from Heaven said: "Both words are of the living God, but only the word of Hillel is the Law." If both words were words of God, then why was only Hillel's word worthy of being the Law? Because the followers of Hillel were gentle and patient; along with their lessons they taught the lessons of Shammai; indeed, they taught the word of Shammai before their own. Which teaches us this: he who lowers himself raises God, and he who raises himself lowers God; he who pursues greatness finds that greatness eludes him; he who runs away from greatness finds that it pursues him. (Erubin, 13 b).

Were the doctors who received Jesus at the Temple disciples of Shammai or Hillel? Did he become aware at this time of the dissension between them? Obviously, we cannot know. Perhaps he met doctors of both schools, but was not shaken in his faith because he understood that different temperaments were bound to make different interpretations of the Law. One thing we can say for certain, and that is that when Jesus was found by his parents and with them left Jerusalem he had gained a complete picture of the Jewish problem of the time.

He had come in immediate contact with the rabbinical tradition of the Talmud and the Midrash. From the talk of the doctors he had gleaned certain words and phrases he was to make his own. The reference to a "heavenly father" was one of these, and it is not surprising that when his parents reproached him for having left them he said: "Did you not know that I must be in my father's house?"

He had also felt at first hand the pressure of Roman paganism. These two experiences, the one of the tradition that holds Israel together, the other of the threat which, from century to century, threatens to tear it apart, were to form the temporal background of his life and teaching. We shall examine them in further detail in order to understand the awakening of his youthful mind and his growing consciousness of his predestined mission.

CHAPTER SEVEN

The Young Jesus and the Talmud

Here is a rabbinic story from a much later time than that of Jesus, which enables us to penetrate the atmosphere of the Talmud, that perpetual commentary of the doctors upon the Law.

Rabbi Isaac Meir Alter of Ger, the outstanding Talmudic scholar in Poland of his day, came to his master, Rabbi Mendel of Kotzk, and asked him to read the manuscript of a work he had written. It was a commentary on Hoshen Mishpat, the Jewish Civil Code. A few weeks later, the Rabbi of Kotzk sent for the author "I have studied your manuscript," he said. "It is a work of genius! When published, the classical commentaries, which have been studied for generations will become obsolete. I am only grieved at the thought of the displeasure which this will cause to the souls of the saintly commentators." It was a winter evening. Fire was burning in the stove. Rabbi Isaac Meir took the manuscript from the table and threw it into the flames.

In the course of history the Talmud has undergone many other burnings. But this one is particularly meaningful, inasmuch as it was voluntary and accomplished by a Jew who was a vehicle of Jewish tradition. It shows that the Talmud never has and never will come to a standstill, that it is ceaselessly in the process of creation. It is not a literary, dogmatic, philosophical or historical work, a treatise or even, in the ordinary sense of the word, a collection. Nor is it "revealed," as are to their believers, the Old and New Testaments and the Koran. It has no equivalent in any other culture or religion.

Hence the misunderstandings and errors of which it is the object, the most extreme and comical being that of the medieval cleric who wrote: ". . . *ut narrat rabbinus Talmud . . .*" (all the Rabbi Talmud tells us). The Talmud is neither a rabbi nor the work of a rabbi. The only modern way to give an approximate idea of it is to call it an "open forum," which goes back mythically to Moses, but historically to the fourth century B.C., with thousands of rabbis contributing to it over a span of nearly a thousand years.

In the beginning, between the fourth century B.C. and the second century A.D., it was an oral tradition, inscribed only in memory and passed on, mouth to mouth, from one generation to another. After this the tradition got into writing; in A.D. 189 came the first transcription, the Mishnah; then, in 396, the Talmud of Jerusalem, which included the Gemara, the first collection of commentaries upon it; finally, in A.D. 500, the Talmud of Babylon, with commentaries more numerous and more important. But if by the end of the fifth century, these two Talmuds were compiled, it does not mean that the Talmudic tradition was interrupted. Wherever there were synagogues and houses of study such as, under the name of Yeshiva, still exist today, the Talmud went on.

In the eleventh century a French rabbi, Rashi, wrote a commentary of the Bible and the Talmud, which was incorporated into its latest edition. In short, no matter how many times the Talmud is revised it is never definitive. It is a mental universe ingrained in Judaism, which constantly develops and renews itself, with all the fertility and diversity of life.

The unique quality of the Talmud is further shown in its page layout. In the center of every page, in large letters, is the Gemara, that is the first commentary of the originally codified Mishnah, or moral law. All around it are the doctor's subsequent glosses, sometimes longer than the original, which serve either to explain its meaning or to draw from it some theoretical or practical moral lesson. "Rabbi So-and-So says" is the way each one begins.

On account of the infinite diversity of interpretations accumulated for nearly a thousand years, it is obvious that the Talmud or Talmuds do not constitute an orderly or logical collection. There are discussions dating back hundreds of years, among hundreds of rabbis, a meeting of minds among men of different temperaments and different periods, alternately of Israel's independence and persecution. The only unifying principle—an all-important one—is that every bit of text is the commentary of a commentary of the Torah.

This common inspiration does not do away with all differences; on every page there are varied orchestrations of the same theme. The general tone is high-minded, but occasionally, in periods of crisis, there are expressions of unseemly violence. In an open-end discussion spanning so many centuries we cannot hold Judaism or its leaders responsible for individual errors. For instance, the Talmud declares over and over its respect for other religious convictions: "It is worse to injure a non-Jew than a Jewish brother." Jews are called upon to love others, laconically, all in the following excerpt: "Who is the strong man? He who changes his enemy into a friend," or in the more rounded sentences: "What is the Torah's message to Israel? Take the yoke of the kingdom of heaven upon you, outdo one another in the fear of God and practice acts of love toward one another."

This sentiment is to be found throughout the Talmud. Rabbi Akiba terms it "a fundamental principle of the Torah," while Hillel, as we have seen, called it "the whole of the Law." Unfortunately, under the reign of the Emperor Hadrian, one of the worst periods of Jewish persecution, a Talmudic commentator, Rabbi Simeon ben Johai, aghast at "the horrible sight of Roman cruelty and destruction," uttered a war cry, intended to rouse his countrymen to rebellion. "Even the best of pagans is to be killed," he said, not meaning to set up a rule applying to all non-Jews, but simply to the soldiers who had perpetrated the massacre. This isolated sentence of the Talmud, contrary to its general spirit, has too often served all a basis for attack against it.

At the time when Jesus went up, all a young boy, to the Temple of Jerusalem, the Talmud had not yet been codified; it was an oral tradition passed down among the doctors, which served as a framework for their diverse opinions, for the fine points of their commentary of the word of God. For this reason we cannot reconstruct the discussions in which Jesus took part. But we can be sure that such exchanges of views became familiar to him during the hidden years, since, as we shall see later on, many of his Gospel utterances reflect Talmudic inspiration and even Talmudic phraseology.

Jesus had not read either the Mishnah or the Gemara, which date from between the second and fourth centuries after his birth. But the fact that in them there are analogies with the text of the first-century Gospels makes for a relationship between the Talmud and the New Testament. They share a common source, a common atmosphere. However the process of osmosis may have occurred, it is certain that the Talmud was a part of Jesus' spiritual heritage. In guessing at the employment of Jesus' early years we must scrutinize both the Synagogue and the Talmud, the two custodians of the genius of Israel and the fountainheads of its legacy to Christianity.

Nothing is more difficult than to introduce the Talmud to anyone who is not familiar with it. Just as the essence of human beings cannot be reduced to a single one of their outward appearances or chance characteristics, but resides in their innermost soul, so the life of the Talmud, a whole mental world joined to the two mysteries of God and God's creature, cannot be conveyed by any simple definition or description.

We must look at it, of course, from a historical point of view. But what good is history without an analysis of the contents such as to enable us to distinguish among the various factors in its formation? Again, analysis serves no purpose unless we explain the method or methods of reasoning peculiar to the Talmud. An acquaintance with this dialectic process is necessary if we are to understand the Talmudists' mentality. Once more we come back to the necessity of quoting the texts, in all their variety of tones, dialectic, polemical, poetical, sentimental. Must we, then, have recourse to a presentation of "selected passages"? We cannot do without them, but no work lends itself less to anthologizing, or is more easily misrepresented by the quotation of mere excerpts; none demands such an acquaintance with the process of its formation and the life it mirrors. To know the Talmud one must live it; it must be the object of total consecration. The doctors whom Jesus met in the Temple had dedicated all their thoughts and feelings to the rabbinical tradition they were about to reveal to him. At this moment he must have begun to glimpse one of the important choices that was to confront him when he attained religious maturity. Would he let himself be drawn into this compact, dense, yet ever-moving world of the doctors or would he, on the contrary, remain outside it and refuse to be a complete Talmudist, taking only from their commentary that which was consonant with his genius and his vocation?

Let us begin by defining the Talmud in objective, contemporary fashion. First, let us consider its vocabulary. The Talmud, as we have said above, is a commentary devised by the human intelligence upon writings inspired by God. Every word and letter of the text under study is the product of a divine intention, which human intelligence is challenged to discover. This pious search has nothing childish about it. The word of God is compared to a hammer, which "breaks stones, causing numberless sparks to fly." It shines forth in a multiplicity of interpretations, which demand a bold, adult effort to pin down the truth. Hence, under the guise of faithfulness to the letter, there is an audacious quest for the spirit. Only faithfulness to the letter can prepare the intelligence to go beyond it; the liberty of the Talmudist does not cast aside the tradition he is pledged to continue. Recourse to word and verse serves to create a code language and at the same time to allow the free play of the mind, liberated from the indispensable signs that aroused it.

Here is a striking example. The *midrash* concerned with the text of the ten commandments notes that the first of them begins with *aleph*, the first letter of the alphabet, in the word *Anoki,* an emphatic form of the pronoun "I"—"I am the Lord your God . . ." of the alphabet, *beth*, in the word *Bereshit*—"In the beginning . . ." To anyone who believes not only in the function of letters but in their personality as well, there is something puzzling about this reversal. Of the two essential texts of the Torah, why should the first begin with the second letter of the alphabet and the second with the first? It is, the Talmudist tells us, the result of a quarrel. For twenty-six generations, that is, for the time between Genesis and Moses' ascent of Mount Sinai, *aleph* protested to God: "Why was not I, the first letter, chosen to head the description of the creation of the world? The *beth* of *bereshit* has usurped my place!" To which God replied that the creation of the world was not the first divine action. Long before the creation there was moral law, even if it had not yet been revealed. In the beginning was the Law, and the world came later. Consequently, in spite of the apparent error of which *aleph* complained, it was really in its proper place, at the beginning of the commandments, which God had carried in God's head before the beginning of time.

Like other Talmud and *midrash* stories, this one is not to be taken too literally. The rabbi who thought up such a fundamentally religious allegory knew perfectly well that things did not actually happen this way. But if the story has no basis in fact, it has, nonetheless, a deep inner meaning. It is important, also, as an illustration of the system on which the Talmud is constructed. Revelation and tradition are not obliterated by the study that grows out of and enlarges upon them. The biblical text is a sacred universe, where nothing is profane or stagnant, where everything is fruitful in spiritual development.

With this living alphabet that transfigures and ennobles each one of its affirmations in almost hallucinating fashion, the Talmud proceeded to build up its various parts, which noninitiates may, for lack of knowledge, confuse one with another. There are two main divisions, of different meaning and value, the Halakah and the Haggadah. The commentaries of the Halakah have the binding force of law; those of the Haggadah are purely personal opinions, for which, as we should say in modern terms, "the authors alone are responsible."

As Edmond Fleg explains it:

> *"In the immense labyrinth of the two Talmuds two main*
> *currents of thought are recognizable. The commentaries of the Law*
> *belong to the realm of jurisprudence and constitute the Halakah,*
> *which has legal validity, that is, on condition that, according to*
> *a traditional interpretation of Exodus, 3:2, they represent a*
> *majority opinion of the doctors who have discussed them. The*
> *commentaries of the rest of the Bible are in the field of the imagi-*
> *nation, as it is applied to a more or less legendary past, to an*
> *imperfect knowledge of the universe, to the need of stirring an*
> *assembly of the faithful, of discovering the mysteries of creation or*
> *anticipating visions from beyond the grave and promises of the last*
> *days of the world. All together these make up the Haggadah, a*
> *collection of stories, fables, dreams, images and symbols, which no*
> *Jew is bound to regard as rigorous truth."*

Between the Halakah and the Haggadah there are one point of difference and two of likeness. The point of difference lies in the fact that all of Israel subscribes to and is responsible for the Halakah, whereas the Haggadah may or may not be accepted, and its meaning is open to discussion. Many erroneous opinions and calumnies on the subject of the Talmud are due to ignorance of the exact nature of its composition.

Aside from this essential difference, there are two points that both parts have in common. First, their extraordinary abundance. The *halakot*, or legal precepts, are so numerous that when Maimonides codified them in the twelfth century they filled no less than fourteen volumes. As for the *haggadot* or, as they are more commonly called, *midrashim*, they make up the contents of a large number of tractates and contribute to biblical literature the world over. The second likeness is that both *halakot* and *haggadot*, precepts and commentaries, come from an interpretation of the Torah made by means of the Torah itself. Their argumentation, which we shall examine later on, feeds on the Law and the Prophets; the exegesis of every verse is made on the basis of other verses. Thus a *halakah* or a *midrash* inspired by Genesis may rise out of the comparison of a verse from the beginning of this first book of the Pentateuch with one from Job or Ecclesiastes or from one of the prophets with which it has an affinity of thought or expression.

The Talmudist thinks only of God, but his familiarity with God's scriptural portrayal is enhanced by flights of the imagination that lead to the discovery of new perspectives on spiritual values. The method or methods employed vary with the century and according to whether it is a question of Halakah or Haggadah. Here we perceive the complexity of the Jewish mind and of the rabbinic tradition that stems from it. It is at the same time sentimental and logical, capable of great impulses of the heart or the imagination and yet attached to the exact and sometimes pedantic rules of an implacable dialectic. For hundreds and hundreds of years an alienated and often persecuted Israel lived in close intimacy with God. Its mental makeup, as seen from the outside, may seem narrow. But if we enter deeply into the Jewish conscience we shall see that its limitations exist only in the eyes of a shallow observer. Actually it opens up to the inside; it is like a convent whose walls seem to shut it in, while all the time it is humming with prayers to God that rise ceaselessly toward the sky.

The double merit of the Talmud, sublime in its aim and worldly in its means, soaring in aspiration and yet bound to the rules of human dialectic, closed on the outside and open on the inside, is particularly evident in one of the doctors of Jesus' time. We have already noted his indulgence and now we must look at his severity. Hillel was not only the rabbi who would have been most congenial to Jesus on account of his broad-mindedness; he was also a man who drew up, as a vehicle for his generous ideas, the most rigorously logical system of exegesis the Talmudists had ever known. Thus he was at the same time a promoter of both free inspiration and disciplined argumentation.

Hillel the Wise is considered the codifier of the Talmudic method. He established or at least formulated rules for the interpretation of the written Law and for the spread of its action. There are seven rules, each one of them equivalent to a definite operation:

> *A fortiori*
> *Analogy*
> *Deduction from one (biblical) verse*
> *Deduction from two verses*
> *Inference from general and particular; from particular and general*
> *Similarity elsewhere*
> *Deduction from context*

These rules, taught in the *Bet-Hillel*, or House of Hillel, which Jesus must have heard mentioned by the doctors in the Temple, were intended to extract from a single verse of the Bible the lesson God had put in it, to concretize, by the dialectic method, the manifestations of the divine in everyday living. The process may seem formalistic, but actually it goes beyond formalism and acquires a spiritual value. It is concerned with human attitude toward the divine and defines the application of the divine, as willed by God, to the universe.

Here, for instance, is an example of the application of the first rule listed above.

The Sabbath, that weekly human reenactment of God's rest after the creation, is the focal point of the Jew's religion, the time when they feel closest to God. In spite of its repetition it is more important than the most festive of the once-a-year holy days, even

Rosh Hashanah, Yom Kippur and Passover. And so, Hillel says, if a certain kind of work is authorized for the Sabbath day, we may presume that it *is* authorized, *a fortiori*, for the other, less holy days as well. And, conversely, if a certain kind of work is forbidden on one of the occasional holy days, it is all the more strictly forbidden on the Sabbath.

If we reflect that one of the essential purposes of the Halakah, the juridical part of the Talmud, is to establish the Jew's priestly duties on the days consecrated to God and if we remember these days' importance for a people who live for God and cannot hope to endure except through loyalty to its ancient Covenant, then we shall see how deep a feeling lies behind these minutely detailed regulations. In the divine service formality takes on a committed, existential meaning. Applied to the living God it becomes concrete and intensely experienced.

This is the paradox of the Talmud, particularly of the Halakah, which lends moral value and transcendent meaning to a human logic in itself purely mechanical and therefore capable of leading to either truth or error. At worst it may bog down in arbitrary conventions, which undermine the foundations of human life and suppress all real contacts between humans and the universe, between God and humanity. At best, if it respects these contacts, it can verify and concretize them.

"It is a mistake," says the Talmud, "in the process of reasoning, to come to conclusions, no matter how skillfully deduced, which are contradictory to reality. And it is an even more serious mistake to come to conclusions that contradict the Law, while calling upon its name. No deduction must be made from the Law that alters the Law."

It was dangerous to be a Talmudist, just as it is always dangerous to apply human reason to matters that surpass it. And particularly dangerous in Jesus' time, when the profane reasoning of the pagan Greeks and Latins was an influence so deeply upsetting. And so in its juridical part, the dictatorial Talmud is full of reserves and scruples. Its apparently solid structure is in reality frail and vulnerable. If its logical rules do not rest upon a feeling for the sacred then they become formal and inhuman.

This great pitfall of the *halakot* was not so evident before Israel was subjected to the pressure of the pagan world. But at Jesus' time, when the Romans occupied Jerusalem, stood guard over its Temple and influenced the choice of its clergy, the legalistic features of the Talmud, cut off from their spiritual sources, may well have had something repellent about them.

The Haggadah, composed of *midrashim,* on the other hand, suffered from no such liability. Like its severe counterpart, the Haggadah is an elaboration of God's word by the word itself. But it proceeds by analogies rather than by logic, in a poetical rather than a dialectical manner. We might describe it in the words of Baudelaire's sonnet about man and nature:

> *He wanders there through woods of symbols, and they gaze at*
> *him with looks he seems to know.*

For the composer of *midrashim* the Torah is a wood dense with symbols, or rather, allegories. The *midrash* is a specifically Jewish creation, in which an event's moral or spiritual significance is as important as its material reality. The whole Bible is, in a way, a *midrash*, for the events that it relates express moral and spiritual values and bear witness to the Law of God. The Gospels themselves, conceived in a Jewish atmosphere, contain *midrashim* in which the early Christians, so close to Judaism, saw a new incarnation of the Law. The parables and miracles of Jesus belong to the Haggadah, just as much as the Old Testament stories illustrative of the divine will.

Let us recapitulate the difference between the Haggadah and the Halakah. "The Halakah," says a Jewish sage, "is the incarnation of the Law; the Haggadah is liberty disciplined by the Law and bearing an imprint of morality . . . The Halakah may be compared to the ramparts of the sanctuary, for which every Jew is ready to die; the Haggadah to the irregularly shaped, fragrant and colorful flower beds which display their exotic charm at the foot of the Temple walls."

Whatever terms of comparison we may use, nothing can take the place of concrete examples. Let us see, then, in what guise the Talmud, both Halakah and Haggadah, presented itself to Jesus.

The young boy, fresh from the provinces, had doubtless never known doctors whose life was consecrated to the study of the Law; he had never penetrated the Talmud, this monument to the rabbinic tradition that was, at the time, Israel's great unwritten religious and literary compendium. How did he react to it? Without attempting a foolhardy reconstruction, we can imagine some of the events of his sojourn in the Temple.

Probably the doctors received him in one of the rooms adjacent to the synagogue, which was secluded and quiet, in contrast to the holiday clamor of the courts outside. This was not a room set aside for study, but on tables or shelves along the walls, or perhaps even in a tabernacle, there were stacked scrolls bearing the sacred texts from Genesis to the Prophets. At intervals the doctors went to look up a particular verse to support the point of view they were setting forth to the boys and young men before them. They were so familiar with the material that they found at once what they were looking for. Latter-day Talmudists have been known to press the point of a pencil against a verse of the Torah and to predict accurately on which word of a verse on the following page it will leave its mark.

But in spite of their learning the doctors were not mere pedants. Representatives of the holiday crowd outside came in at intervals to interrupt them. A beggar implored alms; a man of conscience came to resolve some moral problem that was on his mind; the head of a family questioned them about the details of his household Passover celebration: the proper hour at which to hold the Seder, the foods to be served, the order of the traditional questions and answers. All these matters were settled by consultation of the sacred scrolls around the walls, for both public life and private life were regulated by the Law. As Jesus approached these learned men he may well have felt a deepening and strengthening of the ties that bound him to the tradition of his fathers.

The doctors, with prayer shawls over their shoulders and prayer vests (*tallith katan*) worn next to the skin, welcomed this opportunity to instruct the young. They were not members of the professional clergy; indeed they had gainful occupations on the outside, for it was forbidden to make money from teaching the Torah. In the exercise of a spare-time priestly function they found a welcome release from worldly cares and also a source of spiritual satisfaction. They were happy to renew their intimacy with God, to deepen their understanding and to carry out the prescriptions of the *Shema* by teaching the commandments to their juniors.

To the young Nazarene their argumentation may at first have appeared unduly difficult, requiring a mental effort such as to bring on tension and fatigue. But their contagious enthusiasm, the joy they derived from the closely reasoned justification of a subtle Halakah, the peaceful assurance that rang out in their singsong declarations, all these facilitated Jesus' approach to the world of their intellectual tradition.

Changing their pace, the doctors allowed their young hearers to relax momentarily the strained attentiveness required by the

Halakah, and listen to the Haggadah. Jesus could not have failed to notice the lesser emphasis they placed upon it. The Halakah, which teaches the practical applications of the Torah or, in brief, of God's word, must be strictly taught, so that there is no misunderstanding of the text.

Let us suppose, since the young Jesus had come straight from a village synagogue and knew nothing of the practices of the Temple, that the doctors chose to initiate him to the Temple's peculiar rite, sacrifice. How many *halakot* they would have had to expound! There was no question of going into all the ritual prescriptions; it was hard enough to describe its origin and meaning. For sacrifice, the all-important religious act that was the monopoly of the Temple, had as many forms as there were ceremonies and almost as many as the days of the year. Although all the sacrifices had points in common, they had also individual characteristics that the famous rules of Hillel allow us to compare one with another.

In the sacrifice of Yom Kippur the essential was the purity of everything concerned, from the priest to the sacrificial object. The Gemara tells us what were the priest's preliminary obligations:

> *Seven days before . . . the priest was removed from his house to the cell in the northeastern corner of the birah. It was called the cell of the stone chamber (Bet ha-even) . . . Because all its functions had to be performed only in vessels made of either . . . stone or earthenware.*

Why the choice of stone? Because the objects used must be incapable of becoming impure. Something made of clay or a mineral directly out of the earth was guaranteed against impurity by the fact that it came straight from God's hand. Conversely, any raw material manufactured by human hands was subject to impurity. But there was no use in assuring the purity of the accessories if the person who manipulated them was not equally pure. The Gemara proceeds more cautiously to discuss what was necessary for the high priest's purification. Was his seven-day quarantine to be shared by his wife and children? Exactly how was the lustral water to be mixed with the ashes of a red heifer? And what was the comparative significance of the sacrifices, that of two goats and that of a goat and a bullock? Like lawyers caviling in their clients' behalf, the doctors debated every detail of the ritual regulations. But here it was a question not of law but of the Law. At stake was not the fate of an individual but that of all humankind, to be settled upon the coming of the Messiah. And the nature of the Messiah's judgment would be determined by the sum total of human actions here below.

We have compared the Talmudists to lawyers. But their strivings were ennobled by a religious motive. Every step of their reasoning went back to the Scriptures: a sentence from Genesis, from one of the Prophets, from the books of Jonah or Esther, all these worked together to hasten God's coming. Such meticulous research was bound to produce a certain number of pedants, but when it was accompanied by an impulse of the heart, when strict religious observance brought with it the spirituality that the Talmud says every Sabbath offers to longing people anew, then the weight of excessive thinking is replaced by an extraordinary feeling of liberty and joy.

To arrive at this point requires a laborious effort. Jesus must have had to strain his youthful mind to encompass the complex and minute reasoning of the doctors. It was at this juncture that their grasp of educational psychology caused them to pass from the Halakah to the Haggadah. The Haggadah or the *midrash*, says one of the Talmudists, is like a dessert served at the end of a heavy meal.

Like the Halakah it presupposes constant recourse to the Scriptures, so that the doctors had to consult in the same way as before the sacred scrolls stacked up around the walls. But in the rabbinic tradition the Haggadah, without any loss of importance, is almost recreational in character. When rabbis teach the Haggadah they are like a schoolmaster giving students a break by telling them stories. What a variety of riches they offer, and what a welcome interruption, to the young Jesus, of the closely knit logic of the Halakah! There are examples of outright joking on the part of sages with a definite sense of humor and often a touch of misogyny.

Why, for instance, asks one of the Talmudists, did God make woman from Adam's rib? Here is his version of the story:

> *God deliberated from which part of man to make woman. He said, "I must not create her from the head that she should not carry herself haughtily; nor from the eye, that she should not be inquisitive; nor from the ear, that she should not be an eavesdropper; nor from the mouth, that she should not be too talkative; nor from the hand, that she should not be too acquisitive; nor from the foot, that she should not be a gadabout; but from a hidden part of the body, that she should be modest."*

Such a theory was bound to engender further discussion. Some doctors espoused the cause of Eve. They praised woman's love of work: "Women do not hang lazily about the house"; and their intelligence: "God made woman more intelligent than man." But others were frankly mocking. They accused women of being talkative: "Ten measures of words were sent down into the world, of which woman took nine and man one"; and of various faults besides: "Women are reported to have four salient characteristics: they are greedy, they listen at doors, they are lazy and jealous. Moreover, they are loquacious and quarrelsome."

Is this mere oversimplified common sense? Not so. These mocking comments arouse philosophical reflections. Usually the

Haggadah is less personal in tone and less ironic; its teachings are definitely religious and moralistic in character. Jewish morality is based on love and mercy, and the Haggadah shows God practicing these two virtues and giving them as examples to humans. In the rabbinical tradition there is a perpetual quarrel between the two divine attributes of mercy and justice, both of which are obviously indispensable to the progress of the universe.

Here is an allegorical story, told in a *midrash*:

> *A king who had some empty glasses said to himself: "If I pour hot water into them they will crack; if I pour ice-cold water into them they will also crack!" What did the king do? He mixed the hot and the cold water together and poured it into them and they did not crack. Even so did the Holy One, blessed be he, say: "If I create the world on the basis of mercy alone, the world's sins will greatly multiply. If I create it on the attribute of justice alone, how could the world endure? I will therefore create it with both the attributes of mercy and justice, and may it endure!"*

But although God may consider both these elements indispensable, this does not mean that God employs them with equal pleasure. God is much happier to deal out mercy than justice.

> *When the Holy One (blessed be his name!) was about to create the first man, he foresaw that both good and evil would come out of him. "If I go ahead and create him," he said to himself, "there will be wicked men among his descendants. But if I fail to create him, then there will be no good men to owe him their existence." And so, what did he do? He removed his thoughts from the wicked, took upon himself the attribute of mercy and created man.*

"The attribute of grace," the Haggadah says elsewhere, "is five hundred times greater than that of justice." A very precise statement, which concludes a piece of subtle Talmudic reasoning. God has declared that God will punish children "for the iniquity of parents, to the third and fourth generation." (Exodus 20:5), but in the next verse shows "steadfast love to the thousandth generation." Now the Hebrew plural, *alaphim*, must designate at least two thousand. We see, then—that if heavenly wrath is visited upon at the most four generations and heavenly grace upon at least two thousand, it follows that God's mercy is five hundred times as great as God's justice. It is with just such a mixture of allegorical tales and meticulous reasoning, spiced with humor, that the Haggadah conveys a moral. Moreover, it contains its share of strictly religious teaching. Numerous *midrashim* bear witness to the presence and power of God. Here is a typical anecdote:

> *A ship owned by a pagan was on the high seas, and aboard it was a Jewish boy. A fierce storm arose, and the pagans called upon their idols, but in vain. Admitting the failure of their prayers they turned to the young Jew. "Pray to your God," they said, "we have heard that he is all-powerful and that he answers the supplications that are addressed to him." The boy responded by offering up an earnest prayer. God listened to him, and the sea was calmed. When the ship put into port the passengers went ashore to buy what they needed. "Is there nothing you want to buy?" they asked the boy. "What should a poor stranger like myself buy?" he replied. "A poor stranger?" they exclaimed. "We are the poor strangers! Some of us have gods in Babylon, some in Rome; others carry their gods with them but have received no help. But you, wherever you go, enjoy your God's protection."*

The Eternal is not only ever-present; the Eternal is omniscient as well. "Reflect upon three things," says Rabbi Judah the Prince, compiler of the Mishnah, "and you will not fall into sin. Know what is above you, a seeing eye, a hearing ear, and all your deeds recorded in a book."

God is omnipotent also. A well-known rabbinical sentence says: "Everything is subject to the power of Heaven except the fear of Heaven," which means that although God determines human fate God leaves people free to fear or not to fear the Almighty.

Such *haggadot*, of varied nature and tone, bring God closer to earth and allow humans to achieve divine intimacy. In the same familiar way they treat the great biblical figures, people who submit to divine justice or are messengers of God's will. They are humanized, but it is for the sake of pointing up their relationship with God. Let us look at the following *midrash* account of the last moments of Adam and Eve:

> *When Adam was nine hundred and thirty years old, and ailing, he sent Eve and Seth to the vicinity of the Garden of Eden, to ask God to accord a dying man some of the oil of life (or of mercy) which runs from the tree of the Garden. The precious oil was refused but Michael told them, in God's name, that after their resurrection Adam and the rest of the holy people would enter Paradise. Adam died, and God forgave him. The angels came for his body and buried it in Eden.*
>
> *Six days later Eve died in her turn; having asked Seth to inscribe the story of his parents' life on tablets of stone and on tablets of clay. "Because," she said, "the Archangel Michael told us: 'On account of your transgressions the Lord will visit his wrath on your descendants, first by water and then by fire.' Thus the stone tablets will survive the flood and the clay tablets the world's final burning."*

This story illustrates in lively fashion Adam and Eve's desire for survival and God's ultimate pardon of their sin. But, we may ask, does it have any other than an allegorical intention? Does it claim that Adam and Eve really acted this way, or are the facts subordinate to some deeper meaning?

Another even more typical *midrash* may answer our question. The subject is the Children of Israel's crossing of the Red Sea, the withdrawal of its waters that enabled them to walk through it on dry land. Is this story historically true? For two thousand years not only theologians but historians and scientists as well have tried to find out whether the tidal movements of the Red Sea were such as to cause it to seem to retire when the Children of Israel reached it in their flight.

To the Talmud this is no problem; the materiality of the miracle does not matter. The important thing—and this emphasis is typically Talmudic—is the meaning God wishes us to attach to the story. According to the Talmud, the passage of the Red Sea is the antithesis of the Flood. In the Flood, God manifested anger at the sinful human race by covering the earth with water. The parting of the Red Sea and the emergence of dry land demonstrated a change of heart. God no longer sought to punish or destroy humankind but to assure its survival. It bore witness to a new pledge on God's part to the Children of Israel.

This interpretation on the part of the writers of the Haggadah gives the episode an importance far greater than its historical reality. It matters very little whether or not actual events followed the lines of the Bible story. The essential thing is that first God and then the people whom God inspired endowed it with a moral and religious significance that strengthened Israel's priestly vocation.

Such an interpretation accords with the spirit of the Talmud, that is with the spirit of Judaism in Jesus' time. The atmosphere in which the Haggadah developed was that of a sacred world, in which words and gestures took part in God's will. Every element of this world lent its support to the divinity. Every historical event, real or allegorical, was a manifestation of Divine Providence. Its terrestrial coordinates, in space and time, might be approximate or debatable, but it was connected to Divine Providence by a direct spiritual line; its spiritual truth was more important than its material verisimilitude.

In this atmosphere, favorable to prophets, initiates and belief in miracles, the twelve-year-old Jesus spent three days as a disciple and partner of the doctors. This sojourn in the Temple must have deepened his understanding of the religious tradition into which God had caused him to be born. An understanding not so much of historical details or of the letter of the law, as of the spirit of Judaism, half allegorical, half realistic, as the *midrash* presents it. For although we may doubt that he was attracted by the legalistic Halakah, it seems probable, from the evidence of the Gospels, that the Haggadah was a source of inspiration for his later preaching.

CHAPTER EIGHT

The Young Jesus and the Romans

Among the conventional *berakhot*, or benedictions, which Jesus heard and doubtless himself pronounced in the Temple, there was one more appropriate to Jerusalem than to Nazareth. This is the second of the benedictions at dawn. The first one is to praise God "who has given the cock intelligence to distinguish between night and day." "We must say this *berakha*," the Talmud tells us, "even if we have not heard the cock crow, for it expresses gratitude for our enjoyment of the light of day."

Next come three blessings relative to human life, a burden heavy and yet glorious to carry. It is difficult to be human, difficult to be a Jew, and was particularly so at this time when Israel had the only monotheistic religion and its people, although endowed with the privilege of priesthood, were subject to persecution. The first of these three *berakhot*, the second to be pronounced at dawn, thanks God for having entrusted the Jew with the sublime and dangerous duty of representing God on earth. There is an optional variation of emphasis, as expressed in the two different forms: "Blessed are you, Lord our God, Ruler of the Universe who has made me an Israelite," or "Blessed are you, Lord our God, Ruler of the Universe, because you have not made me a heathen."

These two versions complement each other, and are not to be regarded as expressions of national or racial pride. If Israel is "the people [who] dwell alone and shall not be numbered among the nations," it is for the purpose of conserving the revelation particularly entrusted to it for the benefit of all humankind. This fundamental blessing is not political but religious, and it was thus that Jesus had understood it when he lived in the village of Nazareth, where there was little awareness of the Roman occupation. But when he heard it pronounced in the Temples in the shadow of Roman might, it took on a new meaning; it spoke of Israel's trials, of its subjection to an alien power and the many dangers overhanging its people.

For three centuries Greco-Latin civilization had been insinuating itself into Jewish life and culture. In the first place there was economic penetration, embodied in the imitative use of agricultural and building techniques. In our day this would be comparable to an underdeveloped country being influenced by Russian or American films. Beginning with the third century B.C. the products of Hellenic cities made their way into Palestine and influenced the life of the local population. In general this influence made for progress, even if the imports were not of the highest quality. They were often inferior goods, which Roman merchants were unable to palm off on their usual customers and shipped overseas. Nevertheless such articles, even if they were imperfect, impressed local artisans and made them improve their technique. Pottery was more skillfully baked and more delicately ornamented, patterned after a Hellenic model. Palestinian craftspeople began to sign their work, and usually the name was that of a Hellenized Jew.

After the material influence came that of the spirit. Not that the Jews were converted to the conquerors' religion; the Romans never tried to destroy the beliefs of the countries they conquered or to introduce their own in their place but used tactics, far more subtle and insidious, of assimilation. They treated the native gods as protectively as they did the native population. By contributing sacrifices to their altars they made them into "satellites."

When the young Jesus came to Jerusalem this process had been going on for two hundred years; the Jews had had ample time in which to find out the cost of resisting the conquerors and the advantage of going along with them. In 168 B.C. the revolt of the Maccabees delivered Palestine from Greek and Egyptian domination, but in the following century the new Jewish state, threatened by the Seleucids, sought the protection of Rome, which the Roman senate, for reasons of self-interest, was prompt to accord. Living between the great Macedonian monarchies of Syria and Egypt, the Jews were important allies. They could serve as intelligence agents, subversives or military auxiliaries. A formal treaty was drawn up between Rome and the Hasmoneans and renewed several times, along with supporting financial arrangements.

Soon Rome made itself into the protector of its Jewish subjects engaged in business in other countries as well. In 142 B.C. the Senate sent a circular letter to various kings and people of the Middle East, recommending to them the Jews who lived in their lands. The Jews, then, could depend upon the protection of the representatives of Rome just as, today, the citizens of a satellite country or a mandated territory can call upon the good offices of the power that has them under its wing.

Such were the advantages offered to those Jews who came to terms with the Republic. Even in this faraway century, paternalism was not unknown. On the other hand, with those who refused to play the game, Rome dealt harshly. The Talmud, whose purpose was to keep Jewish religious thought alive, is full of references to the clandestine resistance of the doctors, most of them Pharisees, less inclined than the Sadducees to accept foreign domination. Here is Abraham Heschel's rendition of a Talmudic story that reflects the atmosphere of the occupation in the period before Jesus' birth.

> *Rabbi Judah ben Ilai, Rabbi Jose, and Rabbi Simeon ben*
> *Yohai were sitting together, and with them was a man called Judah*
> *ben Gerim. Rabbi Judah opened the discussion and said: "How*
> *fine are the works of the Romans! They have made roads and*
> *marketplaces, they have built bridges, they have erected bathhouses."*
>
> *Rabbi Jose was silent. Then Rabbi Simeon ben Yohai replied*
> *and said:*
>
> *"All that they made they made for themselves. They made*
> *roads and market places to put harlots there; they built bridges to*
> *levy tolls for them; they erected bathhouses to delight their bodies."*
>
> *Judah ben Gerim went home and related to his father and*
> *mother all that had been said. And the report of it spread until it*
> *reached the government. Decreed the government:*
>
> *"Judah who exalted us shall be exalted; Jose who was silent*
> *shall go into exile; Simeon who reviled our work shall be put to*
> *death."*
>
> *When Rabbi Simeon heard of the decree, he took his son*
> *Rabbi Eleazar with him and hid in the House of Learning. And*
> *his wife came every day and brought him stealthily bread and a*
> *jug of water. When Rabbi Simeon heard that men were searching*
> *for them and trying to capture them, he said to his son:*
>
> *"We cannot rely upon a woman's discretion, for she can easily*
> *be talked over. Or perhaps she may be tortured until she discloses*
> *our place of concealment."*
>
> *So they went together into the field, and hid themselves in a*
> *cave, so that no one knew what had become of them. And a mira-*

cle happened: a carob tree grew up inside the cave and a well of water opened, so that they had enough to eat and enough to drink. They took off their clothes and sat up to their necks in sand. The whole day they studied Torah. And when the time for prayer came, they put their clothes on and prayed, and then they put them off and again dug themselves into the sand, so that their clothes should not wear away. Thus they spent twelve years in the cave.

When the twelve years had come to an end, Elijah the prophet came and, standing at the entrance of the cave, exclaimed: "Who will inform the son of Yohai that the emperor is dead and his decree has been annulled?"

When they heard this, they emerged from the cave. Seeing the people plowing the fields and sowing the seed, they exclaimed:

"These people forsake eternal life and are engaged in temporary life!"

Whatever they looked upon was immediately consumed by the fire of their own eyes. Thereupon a voice from heaven exclaimed: "Have you emerged to destroy My world? Return to your cave!"

So they returned and dwelled there another twelve months; for they said, the punishment of the wicked in hell lasts only twelve months.

When the twelve months had come to an end, the voice was heard from heaven saying: "Go forth from your cave!"

Thus they went out. Wherever Rabbi Eleazar hurt, Rabbi Simeon healed. Said Rabbi Simeon: "My son, if only we two remain to study the Torah, that will be sufficient for the world."

It was the eve of the Sabbath when they left the cave, and as they came out they saw an old man carrying two bundles of myrtle in his hand, a sweet-smelling herb having the perfume of paradise.

"What are these for?" they asked him. "They are in honor of the Sabbath," the old man replied.

> *Said Rabbi Simeon to his son: "Behold and see how dear*
> *God's commands are to Israel . . ."*
> *At that moment they both found tranquillity of soul.*

This extraordinary *mashal*, this significant and poetic parable, like many another Talmudic story, has two levels of meaning. It is not only an allegory; it is also a documentary account of a kind of underground resistance, very much like that of our own day. And there are other Talmudic texts that supplement this picture of the clandestine activities whose tradition Jesus must have known, at least by hearsay. His own time was not one of persecution. The Romans of his day bore down only upon those who openly defied them, and behaved in stolidly "correct" fashion toward the peaceful bulk of the population.

But the memory of the trials endured by previous generations and of the heroic deeds of the resistance movement were still very much alive. There was a genuine fear that the Roman rulers might return to their former brutality, and when the young Jesus came to the official sanctuary of the Jewish religion he must have breathed an air redolent of the persecutions of the past and those of the future.

The Talmudic tradition was rich in allusions to the Roman conquerors, in subtly mocking stories that hinted at means of evading their will. The name of the Romans was not openly pronounced, but as during all other occupations there were many nicknames and roundabout phrases for designating the foe. The Talmud speaks most often of "Edom" instead of Rome. And when the doctors winkingly referred to the "reed animals," they meant, of course, the Romans. Who but a Talmudist could have understood the etymological basis of this mockery? Some of them held that "reed animal" meant one whose good deeds could all be written down with a single reed, or pen, because the Romans' only original contribution to humanity was the respect they bore their parents. Others said that, among civilized people, only the Romans had recourse, in recording their deeds, to a foreign pen, since unlike both Greeks and Jews they had no writing of their own but had to borrow from abroad.

A sensitive boy, and one with a religious bent, could not fail to be thrilled by learning the ruses to which the Jewish faith owed its survival. A clandestine religion has its tricks, just like any other clandestine organization, and the Jews transmitted political news and instructions by cryptic messages. In the second century A.D., when the Romans, in the attempt to impose their calendar upon the Jews, forbade them to go by the dates of their own, Rabbi Judah the Prince, compiler of the Mishnah, sent an emissary, Hiyya, to En-Tob to convey the news in the enigmatic sentence: "May David, King of Israel, live forever!" This happened after Jesus' time, but the method was obviously one of long-standing in the history of the persecution endured by the Jews. Similar conventional phrases were used to rally the people to a religious celebration. "Windmills are whirring at Burni" was an invitation to a circumcision; "Light is shining at Berul-Hayil" to a wedding banquet.

At other times the rabbis, like the inhabitants of any occupied country, turned the conquerors' prescriptions to their own advantage. When the Romans forbade the doctors to carry out the ceremony of investiture, threatening death to the participants and destruction to the locality where it took place, Judah ben Baba proceeded to consecrate five new doctors on a mountainous spot midway between Usha and Shefaram, so that both towns should be saved from retaliation, and only he and his followers have to pay.

Even the observance of religious holidays was altered in order to deceive the persecutors. In some years the celebration of Yom Kippur was not held on the date prescribed by the Torah but postponed until the following Sabbath. From a spiritual point of view this was not a grave lapse, since penitence is timely at any season. The same thing occurred on the day of Hanukkah, the commemoration of the victory of the Maccabees, which could not but be displeasing to the Romans. Custom demanded that for eight days all Jews hang lamps on the outside of their front door. But in order to elude the vigilance of the Roman police, the Jews were authorized to keep the lamps burning on a table inside the house.

The *mezuzah*, the parchment declaring the unity of God that, according to the Torah, was to be affixed to the doorpost of every house and signify its religious allegiance, was camouflaged lest it facilitate the early-morning police raids so familiar to every occupied country. Instead of being displayed on the outside it was hung inside, or even hidden in a hollow tube. The Mishnah and the Talmud bear witness to the fact that a number of *halakhot,* or legal prescriptions, were modified in the same way, in order to stave off persecution.

This tradition of pursuit and evasion, which preceded Jesus and continued after him, was doubtless passed down in the stories told by his elders. Jesus did not know of such things by hearsay alone. During his youth more than one dramatic incident caused an upheaval among his countrymen and subjected him to a traumatic experience such as, in the course of history, many a young Jew has known. For instance, in the year A.D. 6, after a census imposed by the Romans, a certain Judah of Gamala and a Pharisee called Zadok incited a peasant revolt, which the Romans had to put down by force of arms.

The atmosphere of the Temple, at the time when Jesus spent his three days there, was peaceful in appearance only. There was order, to be sure, like the order of conquered Warsaw, nineteen hundred odd years later, but it was order imposed by idolatrous conquerors. The Roman influence was political and spiritual at the same time.

Politically, the situation of Palestine was not unlike that of Vichy France. The high priest was, to all intents and purposes, a creature of the Romans; their governors superintended, revised or annulled his most important decisions. He could not even put on his vestments without their authorization, since they were kept in the Tower of Antonia and brought out only on festive occasions. This humiliating procedure was enforced during the whole of Jesus' life; it was only in A.D. 36, after the removal of Pontius Pilate, that it was abrogated. On the occasion of the Passover celebration, which was taking place when Jesus spent the three days in the Temple, this fact must have been very much under discussion. When the Pharisee doctors saw the regalia of the high priest they doubtless commented upon the fact that it was enjoying only provisory liberty.

The Sanhedrin, which exercised both political and religious power, was made up of conformists. There was a majority of aristocrats among its members, and they were naturally prone to support the established order. This explains the role of the Sanhedrin and of Caiphas in the trial of Jesus.

The general situation was one difficult for the Jews to endure. As the German Jewish historian Graetz, tells us: "The sufferings caused by the pitiless tyranny of the Roman rulers, the heedlessness of the Herodian princes, the cowardice of the Jewish aristocracy, the sycophancy of the high priests and the discard among the various parties" were disturbing to all consciences. Among the upper class there were many who let themselves be bought over; the poor, on the other hand, lulled their despair with the hope of a Messiah. There was also a group that tried to achieve a synthesis between the Torah and Hellenic culture. This group was particularly susceptible to Roman influence.

The attitude of the doctors seems to have been ambivalent. Upon certain occasions they condemned Greco-Roman culture completely and demanded that the faithful steer clear of it. One of the rabbis of the Talmud exclaims vehemently: "Cursed be the man who brings up his children like swine, and cursed be he who teaches his son the lore of the Greeks." Moreover, devout Jews took precautions, some of them extraordinarily drastic, to protect their sacred heritage from pagan profanation. Certain writers believe that the prohibition of pronouncement of the Tetragrammaton, the mystical word that evoked the name of the Divinity, was due to considerations of this kind. Idolaters had made gross fun of it; a witty Egyptian, for instance, compared Yahweh to the Copt word *iw* or *aw*, meaning "donkey." This juxtaposition of the holy name with that of an unclean animal was intolerable. At first the Jews restricted its use to ceremonies taking place in the Temple, then they sought to make it inaudible to the faithful by covering it with the priests' chants. Finally Simon the Just, a contemporary of Alexander the Great, forbade it completely. Substitutes—*Ha-Shem* (the Name) and *Adonai* (the Lord)—were pressed into use. By reason of its absence the Tetragrammaton began to acquire mystical power. The Old Testament book of Enoch tells of the belief that the world was created by virtue of this hidden name, which even the angels did not learn until they had passed through a long novitiate. Thus a whole symbolism was born of the crude pun of an Egyptian idolater.

But although the Jewish sages wished to preserve the Torah from foreign contamination they favored making it known abroad, so that pagans might become acquainted with monotheism. This fact is witnessed by the Greek translation made for the benefit of the Jews of Alexandria.

Alexandria was the city with the largest number of Jews in Egypt, with Heliopolis coming after. In 312 B.C., Ptolemy I captured Jerusalem and took back to his own country, especially to Alexandria, a whole Jewish colony. "Having found them to be loyal and courageous allies he allowed the Jews to settle in a section of the new city and to enjoy the same rights as the Greeks." As further immigration and growing prosperity caused their numbers to increase, Alexandria became a Jewish spiritual center, second only to Jerusalem, in the ancient world. Jews from Alexandria eventually settled in places as far away as Cyrene, in North Africa, and the vicinity of Ethiopia.

About a hundred and fifty years after the settlement was established in Alexandria, a second group of Jews settled in Heliopolis. Most of them came straight from Palestine, where there was at this time much persecution, and they were seeking religious freedom. With them they brought the Pharisaic tradition. Whereas the Jews of Alexandria had become Hellenized, the newcomers for a long time avoided contact with the Greeks and their culture. At Heliopolis there was a definite policy of maintaining the purity, or rather the isolation of Jewish religious thought.

Meanwhile the older and larger Jewish colony in Alexandria represented two-fifths of the city's population. Its continued presence and growth testified to the fact that it was at home in the midst of a Hellenic civilization. At the same time the Jews' loyalty to their own faith and practices inspired respect among their Greek fellow citizens. "The fame of our laws was widespread," wrote the Hellenized Jew Philo. "Some people found it strange that the Greeks should not be acquainted with them at firsthand and wished to translate them. The most celebrated of kings took it upon himself to see that this good work was done." Just as Greek culture won over the victorious Romans, so a Jewish minority influenced the conquering Greeks. The beliefs and customs of the Jews, their concepts of monotheism and moral law so impressed the Greco-Egyptians that their king wished them to possess the text of the biblical revelation.

At the suggestion of the keeper of the royal library, which contained a collection, extraordinary for the age, of two hundred thousand volumes Ptolemy II, known as Philadelphus, wrote to Eleazer, the high priest at Jerusalem, to ask him to authorize a translation of the Law. He declared himself ready, in return, to free a hundred thousand Jews consigned by his father, Ptolemy I, to captivity, by this means, "demonstrating his pity and the gratitude he felt toward the supreme God to whom he owed the prosperity of his kingdom." Eleazar was to send seventy-two elders, six from each tribe of Israel, "selected for their wisdom and their perfect knowledge of both Hebrew and Greek," to do the translation.

When the seventy-two translators arrived at Alexandria the king offered them a banquet that lasted no less than seven days, on each one of which he questioned ten of their number and expressed his admiration for their learning, not only in the fields of morals and philosophy but in that of politics as well. After this they were sent to the island of Pharos, where they proceeded in peace and quiet to translate the holy books. In seventy-two days their work was done, and read aloud before the Jewish colony of Alexandria, which gave it full approval. Cursed were those who would alter this text.

But although the seventy-two sages meant their Greek version to have the same infallibility as the God-inspired Hebrew original, they were unintentionally guilty of making many alterations. Of course it was still the Bible, the Sepher Torah, or Pentateuch, and the Prophets. But although the facts were there, the spirit in which they were told was different. Consciously or unconsciously the Jews were affected by the Hellenized atmosphere of Egypt. Their alterations fell into two main categories.

First, under Greco-Roman religious influence, they diluted the meaning of the Jewish faith. Second, under the influence of Greek philosophy, they bowdlerized both the Bible's narrative and its teaching.

The Jewish faith does not seek primarily to console people for the fatalities inherent in their human condition. It teaches people to accept and grapple with them. It is a clear-eyed view, often tragic in character, which does not seek to hide their harshness and apparent injustice but points out what effort can be made to overcome them.

It is perhaps in the Book of Job that we see most clearly the existential character of Judaism. As his three friends are trying to console the unjustly smitten Job, God makes a last personal appearance in the Bible and disdainfully refutes them. People must not be consoled by high-sounding platitudes, God says; rather, men and women must be put in their place in creation and made to participate in the cosmic order, even if the place is unsure and uncomfortable and the order often seems oppressive. This close link between Divine Providence and earthly reality is what we mean by Jewish existentialism. But what happens to it in the Septuagint version?

To begin with, the Greek version of the Book of Job is one-fifth shorter than the Hebrew original; the translators made, if not a "digest," certainly an abridgment. They suppressed everything which, in the light of their rhetorical training, seemed unnecessary to understanding the text, all the parallel constructions, repetitions and the almost panting rhythm proper to Hebrew lyric poetry. Hebrew lyricism consists of a whole orchestration of echoes around a central idea, an idea that moves forward by dint of alternate contrasts and comparisons, in an atmosphere propitious to the enouncement of a central truth. The translators of the Septuagint were ruled by reason and logic rather than sensibility; they sought to obtain clarity rather than intensity of feeling, and so they did not hesitate to cut out what seemed to them useless excrescences. How shocking, for instance, that Job should speak to God in these terms:

> *Is it good unto you that you should oppress, that you should despise the work of your hands, and shine upon the counsel of the wicked?*
>
> *Do you have eyes of flesh? Or do you see as people see?*

In the Septuagint version, these apostrophes are abbreviated and watered down; indeed, there is a complete reversal of meaning in the sentence: "Is it agreeable to you that I should commit iniquity?" Likewise Job's angry protest: "He destroys the perfect and the wicked," is changed into the ineffective and erroneous statement: "His wrath destroys the great and the powerful."

As the writers of the book from which we have drawn some of the material above put it: "The dramatic debate between Job and God loses all its sharpness. Job is no longer the unjustly tortured innocent man who dares ask the Lord for an accounting; he is a model of patience and humility."

And there are many other examples. The 25th chapter of Isaiah begins thus:

> *O Lord, you are my God; I will exalt you, I will praise your name; for you have done wonderful things; your counsels of old are faithfulness and truth.*
>
> *For you have made of a city a heap; of a defensed city a ruin: a palace of strangers to be no city; it shall never be built.*
>
> *Therefore the strong people will glorify you and the city of the terrible nations will fear you.*
>
> *For you have been a strength to the poor, a strength to the needy in his distress, a refuge from the storm, a shadow from the heat, when the blast of the terrible ones is as a storm against the wall.*

*You shall bring down the noise of strangers, as the heat in a
dry place; even the heat with the shadow of a cloud: The branch of
the terrible ones shall be brought low.*

This passionate and colorful outburst is feebly rendered by the
Septuagint as follows:

*O Lord, you are my God; I will exalt you, I will praise your
name; for you have done wonderful things, plans formed of old,
faithful and sure.*

*For you have made the city a heap, the fortified city a ruin;
the palace of aliens is a city no more, it will never be rebuilt.*

*Therefore strong peoples will glorify you; cities of ruthless
nations will fear you.*

*For you have been a refuge to the poor, a refuge to the needy
in their distress, a shelter from the rainstorm and a shade from the
heat. When the blast of the ruthless was like a winter rainstorm,
the noise of aliens like heat in a dry place, you subdued the heat
with the shade of a clouds; the song of the ruthless was stilled.*

A comparison of these two texts cannot but lead us to agree
with the authors of the book quoted above, when they say that "a
series of slight but definite modifications have altered the general
tone." The Hellenized translators did not only shorten and water
down the Hebrew text; they were unfaithful to its spirit as well.
Treating Moses as if he were a Hebrew Plato, they adapted the
naive but meaningful Old Testament stories to the tenets of Greek
idealism. Even at the very beginning of Genesis we can see the
same thing. The Hebrew text shows God creating out of nothing
the different elements of the universe. Vegetation and trees God
created with particular and truly divine simplicity:

*And God said, Let the earth bring forth grass, the herb yield-
ing seed, and the fruit tree yielding fruit after his kind, whose seed
is in itself, upon the earth, and it was so.*

> *And the earth brought forth grass, and herb yielding seed after*
> *his kind, and the tree yielding fruit, whose seed was in itself, after*
> *his kind: and God saw that it was good.*

But the Septuagint translators found this process too direct.
God was no Aristotelian and did not seem to know the difference
between potential being and actual being. And so they proceeded
to make up for God's insufficiency by giving the text a philosophical
slant.

> *Then God said, "Let the earth put forth vegetation: plants*
> *yielding seed, and fruit trees of every kind on earth that bear fruit*
> *with the seed in it." And it was so.*
> *The earth brought forth vegetation: plants yielding seed of*
> *every kind, and trees of every kind bearing fruit with the seed in*
> *it. And God saw that it was good.*

In other words, God made the images or prototypes of things
before making the things themselves and the act of creation consisted of nothing more than a passage from virtual to actual existence.

The Holy Scriptures, falsified at first contact by the Greek spirit, continued to suffer from its inroads in the years that followed.
At the time of Jesus, Philo, the Jewish philosopher of Alexandria,
carried the idealization of God a step farther. "God seems to me,"
he said, "to have two temples: one of them is the universe, with
God's firstborn, the Word, as its high priest; the other is the rational
soul, whose priest is the real man. The priest who offers up prayers
and sacrifices in our country, in Jerusalem, is only his perceptible
image."

How can it be said that the flesh-and-blood Jew of Palestine is
only a "perceptible image"? No one but Hellenized Jews could
hope to understand. For them the real man was not made of flesh
and blood; he was a disincarnate being.

This is but one example of Philo's idealization of the miraculous yet down-to-earth Bible stories. In the history of the patriarchs Philo saw only an allegorical description of various spiritual conditions. Once more, facts were swept aside to make place for notions and ideas. God's covenant with the Children of Israel was not looked upon as a *berith*, a concrete agreement; it became an intellectual concept, an abstract bond, which provided material for theological study but did not influence everyday life.

This is what happened to Palestinian Judaism under the influence of Greek philosophy. Even forms of worship were affected. The great holy days, instead of being reconstructions of past events, took on a philosophical meaning. As André Néher has put it, "Some Jews succumbed to the temptation of allegorizing the Mosaic Passover. Philo of Alexandria, the leading interpreter of Hellenistic Judaism, explained the exodus in idealistic terms. To go out of Egypt, he said, meant to overcome matter, to accede to the universe of the soul, to make the mysterious transition from the somatic to the pneumatic state." Admirable subtleties! But for André Néher, who is not devoid of malice, and for the Palestinian Jews, to go out of Egypt has still another meaning, and one which Philo did not guess; it means, quite simply, to achieve liberation.

During Jesus' three days in the Temple he did not see the Septuagint version of the Holy Scriptures. The doctors did not expound Greek idealism; their talk was not of Plato but of Moses. And even at this early date Jesus probably showed that he had ideas of his own. At twelve years of age, Greco-Latin intellectual influence was beyond his understanding, and he probably learned more from what he saw and heard than from any number of books. Even so the presence of the Romans must have made a vivid impression upon him.

Beside the Roman soldiers and bureaucrats, he must have been aware of the constant stream of visitors from Italy, Alexandria and Heliopolis. As always, when a nation with an old culture is conquered and occupied there are, among the conquerors, admirers who pay it a not totally disinterested homage. In the outer courts of the Temple there must have been foreign hangers-on who knew the Hebrew language or admired the Hebrew faith and were willing to be instruments of Roman penetration. Roman students of the Torah and the Talmud were enabled by the occupation to meet at firsthand the doctors of the Law. Probably they addressed them with a mixture of intellectual deference and military bravado.

On the other hand, many more Romans showed hostility or contempt for the Jewish religion. It was a well-known fact that the Emperor Augustus had congratulated his grandson for not having gone out of his way to visit the Temple of Jerusalem. In his wish to centralize in his palace the religious life of all the countries conquered by Rome the emperor seemed to consider the Temple "a suspect municipal sanctuary."

But what must have shocked the doctors more than any rebuff to their own beliefs was the nature of the Roman religion to which they were called upon to defer. No monotheist could fail to be horrified upon hearing that a hundred years before the birth of Jesus, the Roman consul Quintus Mutius Scaevola had proposed to divide the gods into three categories: those invented by poets, those conceived by philosophers, and those whose worship had been installed by politicians. To any Jew it was a double profanation to separate divinity into categories dependent upon the social or intellectual class of the worshiper.

Among the Romans, religion came to be the most reliable government police. The Latins, with their analytical spirit, fitted their gods to the needs they were called upon to fill. As for foreign gods, they were made into allies or satellites of the Romans; every conquered city gave its gods to the conquerors. The Romans attached something sacred to these cities the gods had built and continued to occupy. Roman tradition had promised Rome eternity, and other cities had similar traditions. They were built with the idea that they would last forever. And so Rome bolstered up its own eternity by adding to it that of the cities it had conquered. Only one city refused to play such a role, and this was Jerusalem, whose single, transcendent, revealed God was beyond the Romans' comprehension and never assimilated by them; indeed, the Jewish God claimed to overtower and supersede all others.

The Romans situated their gods in space, within the walls of conquered cities. By such localization they thought to obtain eternity. To the Jews, on the contrary, eternity had nothing to do with any earthly locality, any situation in space. They incarnated eternity in history and conceived it in time. The Roman religion was not universal; it was nationalistic and annexationist. The multiplicity of foreign gods was favorable to religious centralization. Only the religion of Israel, the religion of Jesus, had universality. Those who follow God's law, even if they do not believe in God, participate with Israel in salvation. Israel had no reason to be swayed by foreign cults, whose beliefs and rites it disapproved, although it did not condemn their believers.

The great scandal of Jesus' time was that the religion of Israel was dominated by pagans and in certain respects influenced by them. By virtue of the occupation the substructure of religious faith and practice upon which monotheism had rested for so many hundreds of years was beginning to crumble. At just the time when Jesus spent the famous three days in the Temple, his impressionable mind must have been struck by the intensity of the clash between the Greco-Latin and Jewish worlds, which was to be the cause of much of the suffering he had to endure as a grown man. This clash also had fatal consequences for the destiny of Israel. It was the basis of the bitter quarrel between Israel and Rome, which was brought about by a new religion, Christianity.

The beginning of Christianity, which may be traced back, in part, to the young Jesus' meditations in the Temple, did not stem so much from a cleavage between Jesus and the tradition of his own people as it did from a conflict between Israel and the pagans.

PART THREE

After Jerusalem

CHAPTER NINE

From the "Kaddish"
to the "Our Father"

OF THE YEARS OF Jesus' life following his visit to the Temple practically nothing is known, and we cannot reasonably hazard conjectures about them. But the childhood and youth of any person, no matter how exalted the destiny, can be to some degree reconstructed on the basis of the social and historical background of that person's times. Hence we were able at least to describe the influences to which Jesus was subjected as a boy.

But after the decisive days in the Temple the historian is faced by a mystery. Within a developing conscience dedicated to God there was played out a drama that is surely one of the most amazing and, in the literal sense of the word, consequential, that the world has known. By means natural or supernatural (here is matter for unending discussion) there came into being a crucial mutation in human thought and in the story of God on earth and God's relations with people.

It is inevitable that the mystery should endure and that it should defy minute analysis. Pierre Joseph Proudhon, one of the atheists most attracted to the person of Jesus, derides those who seek to reduce the events of his life to everyday dimensions. It would be ridiculous, he says, to ask whether the disciples ate with forks at the Last Supper.

Let us not be guilty of any such absurdity. When it comes to the last of the hidden years we should be concerned less with facts, impossible to ascertain, than with the direction and significance of Jesus' spiritual itinerary. This can be traced, however imperfectly, only by a continued examination of the circumstances surrounding a young Jew of his time. There are two facts—both of them controversial—to guide us.

The first of these is the discovery of the Dead Sea Scrolls, which prove that during Jesus' life certain Jewish groups—either belonging to the sect of the Essenes or inspired by it—lived in cloistered religious communities. Troubled by the religious crisis we have described in the preceding chapter, they announced the coming of a "New Covenant" and set up a rule of life similar to that later adopted by Christian religious orders. Poverty, chastity, baptism, communal meals, abandonment of the sacrifices in the Temple and the cultivation of inner devotion—these precepts were formulated by the "Teacher of Righteousness," whom we may be tempted to regard as a forerunner of Jesus as the Christ or Messiah. Many of his followers lived a definitely ascetic existence in something like monasteries; others were married and lived in the world, constituting a sort of "Third Order," less strict but bound by the same moral laws and participating in the same hope of a "New Covenant."

Did Jesus know the Dead Sea monasteries at firsthand, or did he hear about them from John the Baptist, just before beginning his ministry? Scholars will have to decide. It is certain, in any case, that the Qumran sect marked a transition between the strict Judaism that Jesus knew during his childhood at Nazareth and the later trend, closer to Christianity, which was in the process of development toward the end of his formative years. Did Essene ideas influence the Gospels or were they derived from them? They are, in any case, characteristic of the times.

From a strictly Jewish point of view the discovery of the existence of these religious communities has renewed one of the problems with which Israel is repeatedly confronted. Because the Jewish religion is that of a living God, because it is written into history, it has always opposed asceticism. A well-known passage of the Talmud enjoins people not to isolate themselves from society. It is by the paths of immanence and everyday living that people are best enabled to put into practice God's law. The rabbi, as we have seen, is not a professional priest, the synagogue is not a temple, and the blessings are applied to all the acts of daily life, fitting them into a religious context, but not transforming their nature or separating them from the rest of the world.

Perhaps, at moments of religious crisis, a segment of Israel is justified in standing apart from a corrupt and hence threatened society, in creating a spiritual reservoir that may make up for the general degradation of the faith. To such a purpose the Talmud gives its approval.

In any case, the least we can say about the Dead Sea communities is that they raised problems of which Jesus was certainly aware.

The second fact, or event, which we can with relative certainty attach to the last part of Jesus' hidden years, is the death of Joseph, the head of the family into which he was born and before the law his presumptive father. It is probable that Joseph died at about this time and that Jesus was called upon to pray at the family tomb. The apochryphal Gospels give the text of a prayer that does not fit in with what we know of the Jewish liturgy of the time and must have been composed later. It is more likely that Jesus said a prayer, dating from the period of the second Temple, which is still said by the orphans of today.

The text of this prayer, called the Kaddish, as we have it, is in literary Aramaic, a language closer than biblical Hebrew to what Jesus spoke. Its intonations may well be those of his voice, in conversation with his friends or in his preaching at the synagogue. The prayer itself is fundamental; it is one that throughout the centuries has been part of the fabric of Jewish life. At one time it was used in schools at the end of a teaching session. Then it passed into the synagogue service, where it marks the passage from one part to another. For two thousand years the faithful have stood up to hear it pronounced, several times over, as a recurrent theme of praise. Later on it became the intercessory prayer a son said for his father, in bidding him a last farewell. At Jesus' time it did not have this particular purpose. But he must have heard it said and even have pronounced it himself when he occupied Joseph's place in the synagogue and stood up to lament his absence. Here then is the text:

Magnified and sanctified be his great Name in the world which he has created according to his will. May he establish his kingdom during your life and during your days, and during the life of all the house of Israel, even speedily and at a near time, and say you, Amen.

Let his great name be blessed for ever and to all eternity.

Blessed, praised and glorified, exalted, extolled and honored, magnified and lauded be the name of the Holy One, blessed be he; though he be high above all the blessings and hymns, praises

and consolations, which are uttered in the world; and say you,
Amen.

> *Amen.*

May there be abundant peace from heaven, and life for us and
for all Israel; and say you, Amen.

> *Amen.*

He who makes peace in his high places, may he make peace
for us and for all Israel; and say you, Amen.

A translation, no matter how faithful to the meaning and even the rhythm of the original, cannot hope to catch its intonation. I should like to transcribe here the first verse, if only in order to give an idea of the sounds familiar to Jesus' ear and tongue:

> *Yis-gad-dal v'yis-kad-dash sh'meh rab-bo, b'ol-mo di'v-ro*
> *kir'-u-seh v'yam-lich mal-chu-seh, b'cha-ye-chon u-v'yo-me-chon*
> *uv'cha-yeh d'chol bes yis-ro-el, ba-a-go-lo u-viz-man ko-riv,*
> *v'im-ru O-men.*

The Kaddish, so commonly used in Jesus' time, as in our own, has more than a retrospective interest, for it is perpetuated in the fundamental prayer of the Christian Church, the so-called Lord's Prayer, or Our Father, many of whose themes and expressions are of Jewish origin. Here we have the transition from one religion to the other, as it matured in the latter half of the hidden years, after Jesus' visit to the Temple.

It has been said that the Our Father is a Jewish prayer, and there is textual evidence to support the assertion. The very first word, "our," reflects the use of the plural form that is traditional in any prayer Jews offer up together. Thus during the Yom Kippur service Jews recite a list of sins all Israel may have committed during the year, even though they themselves are not guilty of these sins. The Talmud explains this habit of collective prayer: "Abbai says: 'A man must associate the whole community with his prayer and say, for instance: "May it be thy will, Eternal God, to direct us toward peace"'" (Berakhot, 30 a).

As we have said, the Lord's Prayer abounds in phrases from Jewish ritual. We shall proceed, at the risk of tediousness, to list them. Actually, every one is so pregnant with religious meaning and tradition that their mere enumeration is more eloquent than any commentary.

"Our Father who art in heaven" is the Hebrew *Abinu she-ba-shamayim*, which we have seen in the translation of the Kaddish.

"Hallowed be thy name" is almost identical with the Kaddish's first sentence.

"Thy kingdom come, Thy will be done . . ." An echo of the prayer called Alenu, which voices hope in the advent of the Messianic era and Jewish universalism: "Therefore do we wait for thee, O Lord our God, soon to behold thy mighty glory . . . Then shall the inhabitants of the world . . . accept the yoke of thy kingdom, and thou shalt be King over them speedily forever . . ."

"Give us this day our daily bread . . ." In Proverbs 30:8 we find: "feed me with the food that I need." And let us not forget the passages in the Torah (Exodus 16:15–19) and the Talmud (Sotah 48 b) concerned with manna.

"Forgive us our trespasses . . ." An echo of the sixth benediction of the Shemoneh-Esreh: "Forgive us, our Father, for we have sinned against thee. Wash away our transgressions from before thine eyes. Blessed art thou, O Lord, who dost abundantly forgive . . ."

"Lead us not into temptation but deliver us from evil," an idea frequently expressed in the Psalms and commented upon by the Talmud.

"For thine is the kingdom, the power and the glory," echo of one of the numerous formulas of glorification pronounced in the synagogue upon the showing of the Torah.

And so we see that many passages of Christianity's fundamental prayer come straight out of equally fundamental Jewish prayers, which Jesus pronounced during the hidden years. Nor is this true of the Lord's Prayer alone. The Magnificat is drawn almost entirely from the Psalms and the Prophets. If we read, in the light of modern criticism, the ritual of the great Jewish holidays we find any number of themes that recur in the Gospels and in Christian liturgy.

There are more resemblances than we ordinarily realize in the dogma of the two religions as well. In the Synoptic Gospels Jesus repeatedly proclaims his attachment to the Jewish faith. This is best illustrated by the passage in Mark (12:28):

> *One of the scribes came near and heard them disputing with one another, and seeing that he answered them well, he asked him, "Which Commandment is the first of all?*
>
> *Jesus answered, "The first is, 'Hear, O Israel: the Lord our God, the Lord is one; you shall love the Lord your God with all your heart, and with all your soul, and with all your mind, and with all your strength.'*
>
> *The second is this, 'You shall love your neighbor as yourself.'*
> *There is no other commandment greater than these."*

Jesus' reply is doubly rooted in Jewish tradition. First, because it repeats two fundamental texts of Judaism, the Shema Israel, which is the cornerstone of monotheism, and the law of love for God and humans (Deuteronomy 6:5 and Leviticus 19:18), which is the foundation of all morality, and second, because it is almost identical with the words with which Jesus' learned contemporary, Hillel, answered the pagan's question about the essence of the Torah. In short, Jesus here manifested both his fidelity to the Law and his acquaintance with the rabbinical tradition.

There are numberless other examples showing the pertinence of rabbinical texts of the first two Christian centuries to understanding the New Testament. The Pirke Abot, the *midrashim* and the tractates of the Talmud, in Jesus' time, had not been put together. But in their orally transmitted form they were the basis of the doctors' teaching.

Jewish writers, ever since the beginning of the nineteenth century, have explored the origin of the Gospels. Here are the findings of one of them, Rabbi Elias Soloweyczyk, on the Sermon on the Mount. Every one of the Beatitudes, which are perhaps the most important statement of Jesus' teaching, can be matched with a quotation from the Talmud.

"Blessed are the poor in spirit . . ." recalls the words of Rabbi Levitas in the Talmud (Abot IV, 4) on the benefits of humility and those of Rabbi Akiba (Ketubot 50 a) on the golden mean.

"Blessed are they that mourn . . ." is reminiscent of the idea expressed in the Talmud (Erubin 41 b) that "unhappiness redeems souls."

"Blessed are the meek . . ." seems to go back to the Talmud text (Sukkah 29 b): "The meek possess the earth and enjoy indestructible peace."

"Blessed are they which do hunger and thirst after righteousness . . ." takes up what the Talmud (Baba Batra 10 a) has to say on justice and charity.

"Blessed are the merciful . . ." Compare with the Talmud (Shabbat 151 b): "If any man pities another, God will pity him."

"Blessed are the peacemakers . . ." Compare with the Talmud (Shabbat 10 b), which calls upon the "God of peace."

"Blessed are they which are persecuted for righteousness' sake . . ." Compare the Talmud (Baba Kamma 93 a): "It is better to be persecuted than to persecute."

"Blessed are you, when men shall revile you, and persecute you and shall say all manner of evil things against you falsely for my sake. . ." Compare the Talmud (Shabbat 118 b), which extols "those who let themselves be insulted, without insulting in return."

That part of the Sermon on the Mount that follows the Beatitudes is equally studded with sayings from the Talmud.

"Rejoice, and be exceeding glad; for great is your reward in heaven . . ." Compare the Talmud (Shabbat 118 b): "It is glorious, and I envy it, the fate of those who are suspected when they do not deserve suspicion."

"You are the salt of the earth . . ." The word "salt" was frequently used and highly significant among the Jews. It was an image of incorruptibility and hence of the permanence of God's covenant with Israel. An indissoluble alliance was called "salted." This image goes back to Numbers 18:19: "It is a covenant of salt forever before the Lord for you and your descendants as well." In the Talmud (Ketubot) we find a very practical commentary: "Every food requires salt for its preservation. Money, too, must be salted if we wish to keep it. But in this case the salt is charity."

The large number of Talmudic phrases scattered throughout the important text of the Sermon on the Mount shows to what extent Jesus was influenced, during his formative years, by the commentaries on the Law. We must look not only in the Old Testament but also in the Talmud for the source of his mode of expression. There are affinities between the Talmud and the Gospels, these two branches of the same tree. Affinities of form, such as we have seen exemplified above, and certain affinities of thought, along with equally important divergences.

Both offshoots of Old Testament Judaism have the same moral tone. In his book *Jewish and Christian Morality* the great Rabbi Elie Benamozegh shows that Christian charity has its roots in Jewish tradition. He quotes the description of God in Exodus (34:6) as "merciful and gracious, slow to anger, and abounding in steadfast

love and faithfulness," and the words of the prophet Micah (6:8):
"O mortal . . . what does the Lord require of you, but to do justice, and to love kindness, and to walk humbly with your God?"
He cites also one of the initiators of the rabbinical tradition, Simon
the Just, who several centuries before Jesus maintained that society
rested on three pillars: the Torah, worship and acts of kindness.

Talmudists of Jesus' time or later, such as Hillel (whom we have
already quoted) and Akiba, voiced precepts of the same kind.
"Love your neighbor as yourself," said Akiba; "that is the great
principle of the Law."

The Christian virtue of humility is Jewish, and more particularly Pharisaic in origin. We have only to consider this one of
many Talmudic sentences, which might have come straight out of
the Gospels: "Remain hidden . . . He that lowers himself shall be
raised up, and he that raiseth himself up shall be brought low. He
who humbles himself here on earth for the Law shall be glorified
in the life to come. He who makes himself small for the Law's sake
shall be made great hereafter."

The content, then, is very much the same. What is even more
surprising, more illuminating of the mystery of Jesus' hidden years,
is the fact that the mode of reasoning of the *midrash* and the
Talmud is carried over into many parts of the Gospels. Jewish tradition was to Jesus not only a source of phrases and precepts but of
ideas as well. He found in it a dialectic form, which remains recog-
nizable in his use of it, in spite of definite modification.

The reasoning of the *midrash* and Talmud has two different
aspects. First, as we have seen, in order to understand a verse of the
Scriptures and to extract its full poetical and practical significance,
other verses, from different books of the Bible, are rallied around
it. Apropos of a passage from Exodus the commentator quotes
another from Job, or the Prophets or the Psalms. He moves always

within the Word of God, without searching for outside references or explanations. In the Gospels, likewise, whenever there is a question of showing that Jesus is the expected Christ or Messiah, the proof is furnished by an Old Testament quotation, found to be applicable to the situation.

For instance, the 53rd chapter of Isaiah describes, without naming him, the "servant" of Jehovah.

> *But he was wounded for our transgressions, crushed for our iniquities; upon him was the punishment that made us whole, and by his bruises we are healed.*

The Talmudists, too, have striven to resolve the "servant's" identity. According to the Talmud of Babylon, he is Moses; according to that of Jerusalem, he is Rabbi Akiba.

When Mark (15:28) says that the prophet was foretelling the coming of Jesus Christ, he is adding another element to the Pharisaic debate. He follows the same train of thought as that of his predecessors, but he comes to a different conclusion. He feels he must prove that the Passion was foreshadowed in the prophetic tradition, and it is by the Talmudic method that he does so.

In the Gospel according to Matthew, when the Pharisees speak against Jesus for his expulsion of devils, he turns their own method of argument against them.

> *But when the Pharisees heard it, they said, "It is only by Beelzebub, the ruler of the demons, that this fellow casts out the demons."*
>
> *He knew what they were thinking and said to them, "Every kingdom divided against itself is laid waste, and no city or house divided against itself will stand.*
>
> *If Satan casts out Satan, he is divided against himself; how then will his kingdom stand?*

If I cast out demons by Beelzebub, by whom do your own exorcists cast them out? Therefore they will be your judges.

But if it is by the Spirit of God that I cast out demons, then the kingdom of God has come to you."

The Pharisees may have quarreled with his conclusion, but they were thoroughly familiar with the method by which he reached it.

A detailed study of the Gospels would enable us to pick out a very large number of examples of rabbinical influence, in content, in phraseology and in argumentation. And this would constitute a precious revelation of the workings of Jesus' mind during the critical last portion of his hidden years.

Everywhere we find Jesus expressing himself in rabbinical style. He used both the parable (*mashal*) and the commentary (*derasha*) to expound fundamental Jewish ideas. And when, in the course of his preaching, he came back to speak in the synagogue of Nazareth the astonishment of his hearers was not due either to his references to the Scriptures or to the language in which he set them forth.

Obviously we must not overlook the startling departure his teaching represented from the rabbinical tradition. The present book is concerned with a period midway between two mysteries, two religions. Our limited purpose is to describe the difference between them and to look (as we shall in the next chapter) into its natural or historical causes. Anything supernatural is outside our province.

The first way in which Jesus did surprise his hearers, who were accustomed to Pharisaic sermons and Talmudic discussions, was in his mode of address. When the Gospels quote Jesus' words we find him speaking in the first person and almost always beginning with the phrase: "Verily, I say unto you," or some close equivalent. No matter how derivative may have been what followed, this introduction represented a sharp break with tradition. The Talmud, as we have seen, is an open forum where the search for truth is carried on by juxtaposing one doctor's opinion with another's. "Rabbi So-and-So says this . . ."; "Rabbi So-and-so says that . . ." There is no question of employing the first person. Opinions are articulated, contradictorily or complementarily, in a never-ending debate, which always leaves room for new entries. In other words, there is no individual source of the truth. The Talmud's teaching is collective, and to the best of my knowledge no selection of excerpts has tried to classify the opinions expressed under their authors' names. The collectivity of the enterprise corresponds with the strong Jewish feeling that the commentary of the Law is a manifestation of the covenant not between God and an individual but between God and the whole community of Israel.

It was, then, a bold innovation on Jesus' part to raise his voice in the synagogue, not in reference to such and such a Talmudist, but in self-expression and the appropriation of certain elements of the doctors' ideas, which he adapted to his own. It must have been a scandal to the Pharisees that he should show a spirit of independence and initiative to which not even Moses had laid claim. He spoke in the Name of God, not through the vehicle of tradition, but as if he had a personal covenant with God. To a Jewish mind these two words, "personal" and "covenant," were contradictory. Suddenly the collective search for truth of the Jewish people had become the enterprise of a new prophet and preacher, more enterprising than any of his predecessors.

The second innovation which Jesus brought to his preaching, as the Gospels relate it, is less easy to define but perhaps more laden with consequences. Jewish biblical tradition does not always feel impelled to pronounce itself clearly on factual occurrences. It considers the universe sacred both in general and in detail, both in the broad sweep of its history, as willed by God, and in every minor anecdote that contributes to it. There is no distinction between the sacred and the profane, between a natural and a supernatural order. There is no isolated miracle; everything that happens under heaven is both human and divine. No atom of matter is without a force linked to universal power; every deed or act, no matter how unimportant it may seem to be, is bound to the cosmic destiny and may influence its development.

The Jewish conception of a miracle is, then, a very particular one. A Jew with a deep understanding of human nature sees every action as both concrete and allegorical, rational and miraculous. On account of this ambivalence a Jew lends more significance to the meaning of an event than to its actuality. The Hebrews who lived at the time of the burning bush or the passage of the Red Sea would have laughed, or rather they would have been deeply shocked to hear that today popular scientists, eager to bolster up religion, marshal facts to prove that such things actually took place or existed.

You may ascertain, if you please, whether or not forks were used at the Last Supper. You may study the rhythm of the tides, the motion of the currents, the annals of seismology in order to explain why the waters of the Red Sea parted to let the Children of Israel go through and then closed over their Egyptian pursuers. Analyze the emanations of natural gas from the vegetation atop Mount Horeb in explanation of the Burning Bush, adduce seasonal rains as the cause of the Flood . . . To a biblical Jew, to a Jew of Jesus' time, versed in the Talmud and the *midrash*, your efforts would seem utterly profane. To a Jew the material event is only the matrix in which lies embedded the precious stone of significance.

Little does it matter whether the passage of the Red Sea took place according to the account in Exodus . . . or whether it took place at all. What matters is that God inspired this story, so that women and men should believe it. It is a *mashal*, or parable, that typical form of Jewish narration, an allegory more real than fact. To a Jew the passage of the Red Sea is not a historical event like the battle of Austerlitz or the retreat from Moscow. It is God's answer to the anxiety God had produced with the Flood. In order to free people from fear, to show them that never again in the course of history would the Almighty destroy them, God brought dry land out of water, just as in Noah's time God had flooded the dry land. Mount Sinai is the counterpart of Mount Ararat; a symbol of mercy after a symbol of wrath. As we have said before, the passage of the Red Sea is the antithesis of the Flood.

Having gained his perspective, let us return to Jesus' preaching, to the form it wore and the essential paradox within it. As an heir to the Jewish tradition, Jesus knew that a fact was less important than its interpretation. But just at his time the Greco-Roman spirit was abroad in the land, the Septuagint Bible was dessicating and rationalizing Jewish religious tradition, and the political turmoil was such as to arouse a presentiment of the coming of God's kingdom. Both Jesus and his hearers were suspended between two radically different world outlooks and interpretations. To the Jews the world was sacred, and what was important was its inner significance. To the Romans it was profane: measurement, logic and all that in the future was to make what we call science held the first place in their minds.

Jesus, whose mission was to extend monotheism to the pagan world, was intellectually torn, and even tortured, long before he was physically crucified by the idolaters. According to the Gospel account of his words, we can see that they unwittingly exposed him to two kinds of misunderstanding.

In the first place, during the early years of Jesus' life, Greco-Latin influence was causing the metaphors of the Holy Scriptures to receive a factual explanation. The *mashal,* or parable, was acquiring what we should call a "documentary" value. Let us take an example from the Psalms. Originally no one thought of taking literally their highly imaged expressions. But as they were read in Greco-Roman circles, their poetical symbolism turned into tangible reality. Purely spiritual sufferings were considered physical illnesses, the vinegar a man pours into the beggar's alms basin became real vinegar given to Jesus on the Cross, and Roman soldiers carried out the casting of lots for his garments (Psalms 22:18).

What happened to the Psalms may also have happened to the Gospels. As a somewhat unconventional commentator of the New Testament, Paul Couchoud, observes: "The multiplication of loaves, which later came to represent the perpetuity of the Eucharist, the miraculous catch of fish, which was taken to signify the netting of men's souls by the Gospel . . . It is useless to enquire when and where these events occurred; they occur over and over, but only as symbols of a spiritual reality."

Now we come to the second kind of misunderstanding between the biblical Jews, from whom Jesus sprang, and the Romans. This too played a part in his Passion. For not only do historical events have a different meaning for Romans and Jews, even the words in which they are described are subject to widely divergent literal or symbolic interpretation.

When Jesus admitted to being "King of the Jews," his Roman judges took it as a revolutionary statement, directed against their own emperor. But to Jesus, faithful to the tradition of his fathers, it was the echo of a *midrash* phrase, which had a spiritual, not a political meaning. If we were to take up, one by one, the expressions that stud Jesus' teaching and that, by the reaction they provoked in Jews and Romans, led to his disfavor with both of them, we should see what different interpretations they received, according to the religious background of the hearer. The appellations "son of God" and "son of Man" designated in the Jewish tradition a spiritual sonship, which was accredited to both angels and kings of Israel, particularly David. It is certain that the idea of an actual divine sonship was unknown in Jesus' time and would have been inconceivable to him; it was utterly alien to the rigidity of his monotheistic faith and its notion of divine transcendence. In other words, it had an allegorical value.

Similarly, the expression "kingdom," as we see it in the Gospel according to Matthew, does not refer to a given moment of evolution when God will reign on earth. Once more, this would be a literal interpretation, consonant with the religious ideas of the Romans but not with those of the Jews.

During the hidden years, this mysterious period of meditation that prepared him for his brief ministry and violent death, Jesus found himself at the junction, in both time and space, of two civilizations. On one side Jewish tradition, on the other ancient Rome, the greatest pagan power of its day. For the first time the biblical spirit came up against the Latin mind, enamored of clarity, logic and practical efficiency, in which religious faith was subordinated to the demands of the state.

Jesus was rooted in one of these civilizations and obliged to manifest himself in the other. Any oversimplified explanation of his inner debate, any attempt to cast the whole blame of his execution on either the Jewish or the Roman camp, is a distortion of its true perspectives and a mutilation of its significance, both divine and human. Jesus' Passion and death came out of the fatal clash of two civilizations. Only thus do they make sense historically and also acquire a deep religious meaning.

Jew, Christian and unbeliever must all admit that in an event of this magnitude, however it is interpreted, imponderables have a large part to play. From the Kaddish to the Our Father, the deriva-

tion, the heritage are clear. But in order to understand the extraordinary role that the last of Jesus' hidden years played in the evolution of the world, we must be ready to believe that they coincided
with a turning point in the story of God and God's manifestations
on earth.

CHAPTER TEN

A Turning Point in the Story of God

THE STORY OF GOD'S manifestations on earth contains two kinds of elements, one human, one divine.

We consider as emanating from God anything that seems to exceed the grasp of human imagination. This means "revelations," those eruptions of unexpected evidence, those sudden announcements of unprecedented but dazzling truth, which seem to surpass anything that a person could possibly conceive unless some outside spiritual force had inspired them. Why was monotheism revealed to a primitive people, surrounded by idolatry? The moral law to people enslaved to the same instincts as wild beasts, except that by virtue of their superior intelligence they had made them more efficient, more murderous? The fact that there were human voices to say the Shema, the great monotheistic prayer, that other voices tamed their guttural accents and vehement tone in order to pronounce the love of God and neighbor, that Abraham and Moses were able, as mere men, to interpret a Law that was beyond their

understanding, that Jesus came and breathed sanctity into the pagan
world—all these are historical proofs of the existence of a world
beyond our own.

Another proof is the extraordinary phenomenon of the *berith*,
the Covenant, which in a world where people, nations and religions constantly perish confers permanence upon its signatories.
The amazing permanence of Israel, puniest, and most persecuted
of peoples, the permanence of the Christian Church, which seems
to share the privilege of withstanding all assaults and surviving all
those who seek to destroy it. . . .

Such are some of the traces of God's story upon earth. But the
trajectory of these divine elements is crossed at every moment by
human elements. Humans, by definition, are mistrustful of ab-
solutes and hostile to Eternity. In order to assimilate and tolerate
them, people must feed on marginal notes to history. They must
cut down the sublime perspectives they cannot hope to understand
to the measure of their trivial anxieties and sorrows. God's story is
too simple; revelation does not allow humans to satisfy their taste
for quibbling. The Covenant is too heavy for them to bear; it does
not offer them sufficient petty consolations. In short, they are as ill
at ease as slum dwellers in a medieval cathedral; they are tempted
to scribble on the walls and to light candles for the fulfillment of
their own prayers. The story of God upon earth is made up in part
of such small-scale petitions and familiarities.

The turning point in the story of God was not, then, a change
of revealed truth; it was a reevaluation of the people to whom it
was addressed. In moments of crisis there rise to the surface of a
person's conscience all the primitive fear and cruelty that for a few
miserable centuries revelation has tried to conquer. He or she falls
from grace and formulates demands that have nothing to do with
the terms of the Covenant; he or she wants to be consoled and

rewarded and made happy. And God, in order to keep a place in history, to avoid being sidetracked, is obliged to make concessions.

God might have done it regretfully, tolerating the things that can not be prevented, making allowances for human weakness and ignorance. But because ever since the beginning, humans have been the agent of God's will, the raw material of creation, the source of heavenly glory, God's problem is how to build on human frailty, to open a new road back to perfection. Every human insufficiency should contribute to the grandeur of God. Every weak and commonplace attribute of human nature poses a new paradox, and from paradox to paradox God's story is accomplished.

At the time when Jesus was growing up, a crisis had been brewing with Judaism for two hundred years. The paradox out of which Christianity was to be born was in the process of formation.

The revelation to which Israel had borne witness burst, as we have seen, upon a world closely bound to the sacred. For two thousand years this feeding for the sacred nurtured the human soul. This is something that it is difficult to imagine today. There were none of the problems or anxieties raised by the conflict between the sacred and the profane. "The universe we live in is sacred," Jews could say to themselves at this time. "Every one of the people we see, the words we pronounce and the gestures we make is in communion with this universe. To be born is to take one's place in this pattern of forces; to die is to leave it behind. But the void from which we came and to which we must return, on either side of the brief moment of awareness which is our life, is also sacred and also bound to God. Without benefit of mythology or anthropomorphism, the universe takes us in when we no longer exist just as it took us before we existed."

At the beginning of the period of revelation and covenant Jewish monotheism was a sort of initiation to the universe, to participation in the life of the cosmos. But by Jesus' time doubt had crept in. One of the chief reasons for this was a gradual change in the notions of life after death. Here is the thread by which we may trace the development of the turning point in the story of God that coincided with Jesus' formative years.

To the biblical Jew of the two thousand years before Jesus' birth, to the contemporary of Abraham or Moses, death meant the dissociation of the elements that go to make up humankind. First the breath of life, *nuah*, not unlike what the Romans called *animus* or *spiritus* and the Greeks *pneuma*, which Genesis tells that God breathed into his creature:

> *And the Lord God formed man of the dust of the ground,*
> *and breathed into his nostrils the breath of life; and man became a*
> *living soul.*

This is something so immaterial that the Jews, with their love of the concrete, thought of it as the actual air drawn in with breathing. Then there is the body, *basar*, the physical support of existence. These two together, *rush* and *basar*, form the unit, *nephesh*, which originates at birth and dissolves at death. The *nuah* returns to God and becomes part of a sort of reservoir of breath, no longer attached to any earthly individual, while the *basar* crumbles into dust. The personality is broken up in such a way that it seems as if nothing were left of the person to whom it had belonged.

But at the moment of death something indefinite and impalpable detaches itself from a person, a third element called the shadow, or *repha*, a sort of sub-being, not subject to earthly laws, deprived by death of all energy, which leads a double existence. It lingers with the dead body, in or near the grave; then it becomes a citizen of the empire of the dead, *Sheol*. And so the *nuah* returns to God in a form inconceivable to human intelligence, the body crumbles and the third element, a barely conscious affair, eludes any anthropomorphic identification. Death is not so much a destruction of life as it is a sort of escape from its framework.

The *Sheol* is neither heaven nor hell nor any other sort of annex or extension of the world we know. It defies any human definition and is, literally, "another world." It is the only place where Job was safe from God's anger (Job 14:13); it is at the bottom of an abyss. "At the summit of the mountain of Zion," a rabbinic legend tells us, "there is a sacred rock, the center of the Holy of Holies, which is a lid over the abyss. At the foot of Zion is the entrance to the land of the dead."

What sort of existence do the shadowy remnants of our earthly selves lead in this desolate place? An existence that defies our human imagination, without pleasure or pain, without the sight of Jehovah and godly works. As Ecclesiastes tells us:

> . . . *The dead know not any thing, neither have they any more a reward . . .*
> . . . *Their love, and their hatred, and their envy, is now perished; neither have they any more a portion . . . in any thing that is done under the sun.*

Life in the *Sheol* is entirely different from life on earth. It is established on premises so diametrically opposite that it is a complete negation of all that has gone before.

Everything does not disappear with death, but everything's nature changes so radically that to humans on earth it is utterly incomprehensible. Human personality and very existence are no longer rational and individual; they are cosmic, communal and beyond the grasp of reason. Individual consciousness survives only by merging with universal consciousness, and yet it cannot be said that with death everything is finished, everything is reduced to a subliminal level, close to complete oblivion. In death people very nearly give up whatever it is that distinguishes them from their fellows, the ephemeral personality that differentiates and sets them apart in the framework of time and space, the bundle of feelings and habits that they need for life on earth but which, when this is over, are so much dead skin to be sloughed off, so much surplus baggage, so much data on an expired passport.

Perhaps, when their breath has gone into a universal reservoir, their bodies have crumbled into dust and the spiritual residuum of their personalities has descended into the darkness of *Sheol*, humans may be said to have fulfilled the *berith*, or covenant, that God made with them. Here on earth the Covenant was hobbled by human pride and passion and the restrictions of a rational framework; after death it may make up a part of the great arsenal of physical and psychic forces that God released at the beginning of Creation and that are necessary to its further unrolling in history.

This, then, was the Jewish idea of death during the two thousand years between Abraham and Jesus. Such a complete renouncement of earthly values in life beyond the grave was conceivable only inasmuch as the whole universe was sacred in character. If the universe is sacred, then to merge with it is not equivalent to destruction; it means simply to escape from a partial and imperfect personal existence and to be absorbed by the totality of a creation impregnated by God.

But as, under the influence of idolatrous civilizations, the sacred character of the world was undermined and thrown into doubt, as people began to believe that the matter out of which they were made had an existence of its own, independent of that of any invisible cosmic power, the prospect of merging with the universe after death caused them to suffer anxiety and despair. They wanted to rediscover in the next world what they had left behind them.

It was then that there emerged a belief in personal survival and in a recompense for both good and evil after death. Quite naturally this belief grew out of a period when the Jews were subject to persecution. It originated inside Israel and created a dilemma. Daniel, a contemporary of the persecutions of Antiochus Epiphanes and the uprising of the Maccabees in 167 B.C., predicted immortality to the victims of persecution and to those who died for their country, and punishment in the next world for the oppressors.

And so, two centuries before Jesus was born, we find signs of a turning point in God's relations with Israel. All around, the world was losing its divine character, and Israel was aware of rifts even within its own monolithic sacred structure. The old concept of death was particularly shaken. There were other changes as well that gave Jesus cause for reflection during his formative years and for the proclamation of new doctrine after he had begun preaching.

Human fate, or rather the human concept of fate, has seldom undergone a more radical mutation. A whole system of morality was affected.

For the biblical Jew there was no individual recompense for good or bad actions. The modern idea of a reward for virtue and a punishment for vice—so very consoling, but in the light of everyday experience so improbable—was alien to Judaism. Jews were aware of their personal responsibilities and of the influence of their actions, for good or for bad, upon other people. But instead of hoping or fearing that they themselves would suffer the consequences, they held, in accord with their notion of the sacred, that everything they did would add to the order or disorder of the universe. As a Frenchwoman, Madame Rénee Néher-Bernheim, has said apropos of the deeply Jewish idea of such cosmic repercussions:

> *Every one of our words, gestures and actions has, of course, an*
> *effect on our neighbor and on God, or rather on the covenant*
> *which binds us to God. It has an effect, also, on the concrete uni-*
> *verse, on all its elements which closely or distantly surround us.*

*Every sin makes a crack in the universe, every mitzvah, or good
deed, is a reparation. Sages say that if our sin-ridden world is to
endure there must arise thirty-six just men (zaddikim) out of
every generation. By their purity they have power to accomplish an
expiation (tikkun) and to put back in place, at least partly, the
machinery which our sins have thrown into disorder.*

This relationship between human morality and the order of the
universe is conceivable only if the latter is sacred. But if the world
is profaned by an excess of reason, fragmented and torn asunder by
blind forces, then personal responsibility no longer fits into any
universal pattern and morality must undergo a radical alteration.

Every action must be individually recompensed; unlikely as it is
in real life, people must pay homage to the idea that wickedness is
always punished and virtue always rewarded. This belief is so illogi-
cal that the only answer to it is a belief in the existence of absolute
evil. Such a development is inevitable. If the world loses its sacred
character, if it is no longer suffused by the spirit, then its weak
points must receive large injections of religious feeling and even
superstition. The Book of Job admits that the just may be unjustly
punished; a few centuries later we have, by popular demand,
promises of eternal happiness and the belief that injustice is committed only by error and cannot endure.

The triumph of the profane over the sacred brought about far-
reaching changes in the structure of the Jewish religion as well. Up
until Jesus' time the Children of Israel were a people of priests.
Everyone, no matter how insignificant or even unworthy, had, by
virtue of the Covenant, a priestly vocation. Other peoples, which
did not have the same calling, had equal chances of salvation. Israel's
universalism was composed of two elements: the central core of
Israel itself, whose immersion in a sacred universe made it the representative of God on earth, and around this core a hierarchy of

other peoples, sharing the same history and the same process of elevation. Salvation was open to all peoples, but one alone was its agent.

This sublime and at the same time worldly concept of Israel's mission as a witness for all humankind was likewise conceivable only in a sacred universe. Once this had perished another form of universalism had to take its place. The necessary transformation led to the Christian Church, to the establishment in a profane world of a mystical rather than a physical community, embracing citizens of every nation. Christian ceremonies are mysteries and elevations; Jewish ceremonies are, as we have seen, moods of awareness and reconstruction.

The Christian paradox is startling and difficult to understand; it involves sanctifying the profane and offering it, however unworthy it may be, to God, injecting doses of the sacred into an inert universe, rays of light into areas of darkness. Judaism is not constrained to make such an effort, to effect such a transformation. Jews know that the world is filled with God and cannot conceive of such a thing as profane reality; hence, as compared to the Christian paradox, their philosophical problems are simple. Israel has the certitude of a permanent, living covenant with God: this is at the same time its privilege and its obligation. Of course, the covenant brings trials and tribulations, which are the harder to endure because they are part and parcel of Jewish destiny and everyday life. For the whole of its existence Israel has been subjected to crucifixion.

At the time of Jesus' formative years two religious tendencies, springing from the same background, armed with the same precepts and responding to the same fundamental need, began to be distinguished one from the other. They differed in attitude toward the Covenant and the possibility of further revelation. Each one has a sublimity all its own and is consonant with a different temperament. Judaism believes in a permanent miracle, Christianity in a miracle that is a high point transcending everyday reality. In Israel there is still something of the biblical spirit, in which reality escapes the confines of the spatial world and leads, without intermediary, to God. Christianity was grafted onto the Greco-Roman world, and in order to rescue the sacred from the profane it needed a God who became human.

Either alternately or together Judaism and Christianity respond to the demands of history. If the hidden portion of Jesus' life marks the indefinable point at which they started to diverge, it is also the time when they shared the same providential mission. The discord was between two religious temperaments. For the Jew, God is everywhere and spontaneously present; for the Christian, God's presence must be won anew every day.

CHAPTER ELEVEN

A New Turning Point

IF THE JESUS OF the hidden years were to come back in our day to his reborn native land of Israel, if at the uncertain hours of dawn or dusk, which bring out the eternal aspect of the Palestinian landscape, he were to tread again the streets of Nazareth or the road to Jerusalem, he would find a world prey to the same anxieties as those of two thousand years ago. Are we not now at another turning point of history, at a moment of confusion, when once more the future of humankind hangs in the balance?

In Jesus' time the religion of Israel had to face up to pagans who, although they did not deny the supernatural, conceived of it in the form of idolatry, who betrayed the sacred but did not ignore its existence. Today the revealed religions of Judaism and Christianity are confronted not with idolaters but with deliberate unbelievers, who officially obliterate the notion of God. Today's crisis is far more grave than that of two thousand years ago. It is a question of whether or not the revealed religions can survive.

What message did Jesus bring to the troubled people of his time? What message would he bring today? What is the spiritual situation he would find if he were to return among us?

One constant: Judaism, the religion of Israel. In spite of the lapse of two thousand years, in spite of increasingly violent persecution and calls to conversion, Judaism remains, a little fossilized around the edges, but fresh and very much alive inside, unapproachable and uncompromising, disdainful of simple solutions, but ready to meet any doubt, any suffering that leads to God. Jews cannot be satisfied with words or illusions; for them it is not enough to wish for God to believe in God, to fear death in order to proclaim immortality. They must verify acts of faith and define expectations. The trials to which Jews are therefore submitted and the effort they are called upon to make may lessen the attraction of Judaism for outsiders, but these trials increase the high standards and stamina of those who are within. Today, as it was two thousand years ago, the religion into which Jesus was born is an arsenal of spiritual strength.

One survivor: Christianity. In the course of two thousand years the religion of Jesus has carried on its historic task: the spread of monotheism among idolaters, the introduction of the sacred into a universe profaned by pagans, with the result that God has been made accessible to those who previously turned away. This vocation, complementary to that of Judaism but not exclusive of it, has further progress to make in a world once more contaminated by idolatry. If Jesus were to return, he would draw upon his Jewish heritage in order to answer the requirements of our times.

And what do our times require? A solution of the fundamental problem of every religion, the problem of holiness. Twice, with an interval of two thousand years between, we have seen a solution. Now, another two thousand years later, shall we be able to solve it again?

The first solution was that of Israel. Since the world in all its elements was dedicated to God, humans were meant to acquire awareness of the divine presence and raise the universe to an understanding of the mysteries with which it was impregnated. Hence the rites and benedictions adapted to every passing moment that is written into history, the reconstructions and reenactments that both commemorate the past and keep it alive, the covenant, ever old and ever new, which links the permanence of the universe to the transience of humans.

The second solution was contributed by Christianity. As Roman influence caused the world to lose its sacred character and a new, profane world took shape, not built upon a divine plan but according to idolatrous designs, it became necessary to intensify the feeling for the sacred, wherever there was fertile ground. Hence the appeal to the supernatural, the multiplication of miracles, the mysteries of transfiguration, which for the two thousand years of the Christian era have kept the God of monotheism alive and indeed carried God's light into realms of darkness.

Now we, in our turn, are called upon to solve the age-old problem. In our day rationalism has attained the giddy height of its power. No longer does it seek to direct religious fervor to the altars of humanism; it destroys altars and religions alike. The nature of the drama is clear, and it is just the same as it was before. There is the same clash as that which Jesus witnessed upon his visit to the Temple—the clash between the biblical concept of the inspired character, both human and divine, of the universe, and the Roman concept of a world of blind forces that human intelligence may discover, explore and harness without ever being able to modify them. To the Greco-Roman, a human is an engineer of these blind forces, to the Semite, a human is one of them, the most active and conscious and at the same time the most frail.

As frail as Jesus, during his early years, when he stood up for biblical spirituality against the materialism of the Roman world, as frail as Israel, which all through its history has kept alive the flickering light of conscience amid a world darkened by idolatry. Is the spirit any better armed, any stronger today?

Two thousand years ago, and twice two thousand years ago, at the turning points of God's story upon earth marked by the Christian and the Jewish revelations, the most sacred feasts were those of Easter and Passover.

There are likenesses between them, but also differences, caused by the evolution of God's story and humankind's in the centuries, stretch from the institution of the one to the institution of the other. They have certain themes in common. The exodus from Egypt, which is the whole theme of the Passover, is a partial theme of Easter. The Pentateuch and the Prophets furnish the subject matter of certain readings in both celebrations.

The difference lies in their presentation, mode of expression and the two religious temperaments involved. During the paschal meal, the Seder, which is the essential Passover celebration, when the family sits down to bread and wine and bitter herbs, these three things retain their everyday character even if, at the same time, they have a liturgical meaning based upon the role they played in the exodus from Egypt.

The Christian Easter is different, and the difference began to take shape at the Last Supper. Obviously this was not yet the Christian celebration of the Resurrection; as far as we know, it was just a regular Seder. Bread and wine were present, but they were consecrated in a new way and acquired a symbolical meaning. The meal was no longer a reconstruction of a historical event, no longer an ordinary meal with an added solemnity about it. It was beginning to be a mystery in which the elements themselves, by means of a transfiguration, participated. The bread became the body of Christ and the wine his blood. The family meal at the family table turned into the mystery of the Eucharist.

Passover and Easter fit in, then with two different conceptions of the sacred, such as Judaism and Christianity, at an interval of two thousand years, represent them. Today, after another two thousand years have gone by and religion is faced with the necessity of elaborating yet another incarnation of holiness we may wonder what new kind of paschal celebration awaits us.

On this uncertain ground the problem of the sacred is visible to Christians, Jews and unbelievers. To the faithful of the two revealed religions it is explicit and receives an explicit solution. To unbelievers it has no name, but is present, nonetheless, in the air breathed by Jesus and the patriarchs who went before him.

When Christians worship in a Semitic atmosphere, similar to that into which Jesus was born, their liturgy sometimes undergoes a transformation. At Nazareth, whose present-day population is Arab (that is, Semite), the Roman clergy has given certain ceremonies a Middle Eastern flavor. Some of the Arabs are Roman Catholics, but like the biblical Jews they think of the whole world as divinely inspired and make their worship into a reconstruction. The Good Friday service, said in the Arabic language, gives a realistic, almost documentary flavor to Christ's Passion. His body is taken down from the crucifix, covered with flowers, carried through the church and buried. On Palm Sunday there is a similar reenactment of the welcome Jesus received from the children of Jerusalem. The Mass is accompanied by a procession of children, with gilt wings attached to their shoulders and candles decked with flowers in their hands, who walks around the church and then go out, amid a joyful tumult, onto the porch. The atmosphere is one of ingenuous joy, and the Arabic language, which is Semitic, also

has a cadence similar to that which Jesus heard in the synagogue in
his day.

At Ein Karem, near Jerusalem, the adaptation of the Roman
rite to local conditions is even more striking. Tradition has it that
Ein Karem is the site of the visitation. Here, where Mary came,
heavy with child, to visit Elizabeth, there are several Christian
monasteries, overlooking one of the valleys that the traveler must
cross on the way to Jerusalem. In one of them Hebrew is the language. The Holy Ghost is called *Ruah ha-kedosh* and "Our father,
who art in heaven" is *Abinu she-ba-sha-mayim*. The Good Friday
service is just the same as in any other Roman church, but it is in
Hebrew. In this land where the tongue of the patriarchs and the
prophets, the tongue Jesus heard in the synagogue, is once more
current among people, to hear it in the mouth of a Catholic priest
is a stirring experience. When I asked one of the monks what benefit was derived from this practice, he told me: "A better understanding of the Gospels. Acquaintance with Hebrew gives new
depths of meaning to the Greek original of the Vulgate."

The Israelis, too, have added a new dimension to their Passover
celebration. There is a difference, of course, between an observance of a strictly religious nature and one that seems to have
turned into a laicized national holiday. The kibbutzim, those collective enterprises that have provided for the cultivation of the land
and also for its military defense, are in some cases religious in character and in others nonreligious.

In a religious community the Passover celebration, held either
in the synagogue or in the communal refectory, is the traditional
ceremony such as we have described as taking place in every Jewish
home. But the fact that the liturgical and the spoken languages are
one, so that the faithful can follow the ritual more closely, makes
for a feeling of special intimacy. The age-old chants are sung by the

kibbutzniks all together, clad in their prayer shawls and a cap, which in many cases is in the blue-and-white national colors. This is truly the "kingdom of priests" heralded in the book of Exodus. During the Seder the prayers and stories of the Haggadah follow their usual course. God is thanked for having brought Israel out of captivity in Egypt and for all other benefactions. Traditional fables are told, such as the one concerning the poor lamb, *Had Gadia*, whose subject is the same as that of *The Wolf and the Lamb* of La Fontaine. But with all this, the rite remains very much what it was before.

And in a nonreligious kibbutz? Because every kibbutz, even if it is composed of nonbelievers, holds a Seder. Here, however, there are no prayers, no references to the Scriptures. The emphasis is on the role played by the kibbutz in the war for independence. As one leader told me: "We are celebrating not the exodus of the Hebrews from Egypt but the exodus of the Egyptians from Israel." And so the Seder continues, on the allotted days, and all the kibbutzim join in, whether in the spirit of the Old Testament or in that of today. Does this mean that the religious rite is laicized? Is it not, rather, that even avowed unbelievers, when they are transplanted to the soil of Israel, are affected by its sacred character?

One thing we can say for sure: the return to the Promised Land and the necessity of defending it have made for a new and close relationship between God and daily life, even if there is no mention of God's name. The Covenant of Mount Sinai, which consecrated Israel to the one God thousands of years ago, has put down new roots, in an age when religious belief is under attack the world over. Have we not here the elements of a new paschal feast, or a new feeling for the sacred, the holy?

For what is "holiness" but a series of victories won by God? God's victory over ever-recrudescent primitive idolatry, that is its

enduring meaning to the Jew. God's victory over the more sophisticated Greco-Roman idolatry, that is its enduring meaning to the
Christian. God's victory over atheistic and mechanistic materialism,
that is the sacred goal for which we must fight today. Even scientif-
ic unbelievers, who reveal to us mysteries they do not ascribe to
God, participate in the second coming. Often they feel a need for
it themselves or inspire the need in others. As long as Christians,
Jews and even virtuous unbelievers fail to realize that they are all of
them alike threatened by the rising wave of idolatry and profanation, as long as there is internecine strife among the revealed religions and the forces of humanism instead of joint action against
their common foe, so long will Israel be persecuted and Jesus
nailed to the Cross.

But if Israel's return to the land of patriarchs and prophets, if
the united efforts of Jews, Christians and humanistic unbelievers in
other countries, aware of their temperamental and historical differences but intent upon subordinating them to a sacred common
cause, are of any avail, then the experiences of Jesus as a child and
young man will take on a new significance. Instead of repeated
intervals of darkness we shall have enduring light.

Index

Other Ulysses Press Titles

FOUR FACES
A Journey in Search of Jesus the Divine,
the Jew, the Rebel, the Sage
Mark Tully
Introduction by Thomas Moore

As the search for the historical Jesus leads ever further beyond the Bible, a new image of Jesus is emerging. In *Four Faces*, award-winning BBC journalist Mark Tully travels the globe to bring together the most current theories about Jesus. Drawing on ancient texts, modern archaeology and interviews with historians, theologians and holy men, Tully paints a multilayered portrait of Jesus. *Four Faces* invites the reader to rethink Jesus and his role for the third millennium. $15.00

THE LIFE OF MARY AND BIRTH OF JESUS
The Ancient Infancy Gospel of James
Ronald F. Hock

Of Mary's biography, the New Testament tells us little. Yet scenes from her life decorate churches around the world and are well known to her admirers. The source of these stories is a little-known manuscript that tells the entire story of Mary's life. Originally circulated among second-century Christians, this Gospel is now available again. Here is the complete text together with color reproductions that illustrate the influence of this Gospel on Christian art. Hardcover. $16.00.

4000 YEARS OF CHRISTMAS
From Babylonian Festivals and Druid Rituals
to Nordic Saints and Christian Celebrations
Earl W. Count and Alice Count

Tracing myths and folklore from the Near East to northern Europe, *4000 Years of Christmas* reveals the surprising origins of our modern Christmas holiday. Here are Bronze Age Babylonians exchanging gifts, early Europeans hanging fir sprigs to renew life and Romans merrily celebrating "Saturnalia." With flowing narrative and decorative illustrations, *4000 Years of Christmas* embarks on a journey across cultures and millenia to reveal a celebration that is at the heart of all humanity. Hardcover. $15.00.

THE LOST GOSPEL Q
The Original Sayings of Jesus
Marcus Borg, Editor
Introduction by Thomas Moore

Lost for two thousand years, the Gospel Q brings the reader closer to the historical figure of Jesus than ever before. The sayings within this book represent the very first Gospel. Here is the original Sermon on the Mount, the Lord's Prayer and Beatitudes. Reconstructed by biblical historians, Q provides a window into the world of ancient Christianity. *The Lost Gospel Q* presents Jesus' sayings in an easily accessible form designed to let all who are interested in his original teachings read them. Hardcover. $15.00.

JESUS AND BUDDHA
The Parallel Sayings
Marcus Borg, Editor

The mysterious and unexplained parallels between the sayings of Jesus and Buddha have puzzled historians for over a century. This book traces the life stories and beliefs of both, then presents a comprehensive collection of their remarkably similar teachings on facing pages. Featuring over one hundred parallels, *Jesus and Buddha* lets you explore the relationship between the West's predominant religion and many of the eternal truths upon which Eastern beliefs are based. The book is beautifully designed and printed in two colors. Hardcover. $15.00.

To order these or other Ulysses Press books call 800-377-2542 or write to Ulysses Press, P.O. Box 3440, Berkeley, CA 94703-3440. There is no charge for shipping on retail orders. California residents must include sales tax. Allow two to three weeks for delivery.

About the Authors

ROBERT ARON WAS ONE of France's most distinguished and widely read historians in the 1950s and 1960s. Twice arrested by the Nazis during World War II, he wrote *The History of the Liberation of France* and eventually served in the government of Charles DeGaulle. Finally, after the Holocaust led him to reexamine his own Jewish heritage and to appreciate the Jewish roots of Christianity, he wrote this early biography of Jesus.

JOHN SHELBY SPONG, AUTHOR of the introduction, is the Episcopal Bishop of Newark, New Jersey. A provocative and controversial historian of early Christianity, he is the author of *Liberating the Gospels*, which recaptures the original Jewish context of the New Testament. His other books include *Rescuing the Bible from Fundamentalism* and *Born of a Woman*.